To TIM,

With Best Wishes,

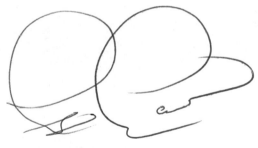

SAN ANSELMO, CA

OCT. 5, 2013

YOKOHAMA GAIJIN

Memoir of a Foreigner Born in Japan

By George Lavrov

AuthorHouse™
1663 Liberty Drive
Bloomington, IN 47403
www.authorhouse.com
Phone: 1-800-839-8640

First published by AuthorHouse 12/13/2011

ISBN: 978-1-4678-7053-5 (sc)
ISBN: 978-1-4685-0299-2 (e)

Library of Congress Control Number: 2011961017

Printed in the United States of America

This book is printed on acid-free paper.

This book is dedicated to my family:
my wife Tatiana,
son Alexander, daughter-in-law Denise,
son Nicholas, daughter-in-law Geri, and
granddaughter Sophia.

ACKNOWLEDGMENTS

I would like to thank Arlene and Kon Balin, whose book, *Born Stateless*, was the catalyst that inspired me to write *Yokohama Gaijin*, and whose support and helpful advice proved invaluable.

Thanks also to P. J. Lenz for taking the time to review my manuscript and provide me with some excellent advice.

A tip of the hat also goes to my longtime schoolmates from St. Joseph, Yokohama: George Belonogoff, for his helpful suggestions regarding some of our youthful escapades; and Paul Uhov, for his expert assistance with Japanese translations.

I also thank Geri Lavrov for her photos of me, Alex Lavrov for volunteering to proofread the manuscript, and, last but not least, Denise Debrunner-Lavrov for the design and layout of *Yokohama Gaijin*.

GLOSSARY

Gaijin: Japanese word for a foreigner

White Russians: Anti-Communist Russians (and their offspring) who opposed the Bolsheviks and fought the Reds in the Russian Civil War (commonly referred to as the Whites)

YOKOHAMA GAIJIN
Table of Contents

INTRODUCTION

The first sixteen years of *Yokohama Gaijin* are set in the picturesque, cosmopolitan port city of Yokohama, gateway to Japan's capital, Tokyo, and now the second largest metropolis in Japan. During that time, Yokohama was a much smaller and more compact city, where you could still travel a short distance and soon be in the countryside. Today, Yokohama's numerous old canals with their barges are long gone, having been replaced with modern freeways and bridges. Still, since I am a Hamakko, a native of Yokohama, a little bit of charming old Yokohama remains forever in my heart. I was born there on March 5, 1941, a time of impending war in the Asian and Pacific areas. My mother, Daria, gave birth to me at home with the assistance of a Japanese midwife—a common practice in those days. While the Pacific war started on December 7, 1941, with Japan's undeclared attack on Pearl Harbor, the winds of war had been gathering for a long time. Foreigners, called gaijin by the Japanese, were departing Japan in order to avoid the catastrophe that everybody knew was coming. At the time, Imperial Japan was ruled by militarists with expansionary ambitions. Their goal was to expand the Japanese empire not only in northeast Asia, but to points far beyond. It is into this dark and dangerous geopolitical environment that I was born, but that was my fate. My one consolation was that I was only four and a half years old when the tragic war ended with Japan's unconditional surrender in August, 1945, and I did not have to endure most of the horrors and tribulations my parents and older siblings experienced during the difficult war years.

CHAPTER 1
May 29, 1945: Target Yokohama

On May 29, 1945, 450 B-29s from the Marianas, escorted by about 150 P-51 Mustangs from Iwo Jima, attacked Yokohama with 3,200 tons of incendiary bombs. Nine square miles of Yokohama were literally wiped out, including the Sagiyama Ridge neighborhood where my family lived. The air raid warnings sounded, and we rushed to a nearby cave that had been converted to a bomb shelter. My older brother Konstantin, who was fifteen, was not with us, but my parents assumed he had found a safe place.

I recall how hot and uncomfortable it was in the shelter, with sparks flying all over. When we were allowed to leave, we witnessed the inferno, which was like an earthly hell. Everything was burning, some of the fires reaching five stories high. As my family and I walked down the steps from the shelter, I saw some Japanese folks sitting nearby. I soon realized they were dead. The smell of burning flesh permeated the whole area, and it appeared eerily quiet.

Our house had taken a direct hit. My brother had not found a safe place; believing it was another false alarm, he had gotten under his bed. Konstantin was killed instantly, a horrible tragedy for everyone in my family.

May 29, 1945, is forever etched in my mind, even today,

sixty-five years later. When I hear a plane aloft in the middle of the night, I immediately wake up and, for a few seconds, relive the fear of that attack all over again. It is my first vivid memory as a child of four.

In this final B-29 raid on Yokohama, and except for our expropriated house, my family lost everything, including our beloved Konstantin, who was buried in the Yokohama Foreign Cemetery. It was a difficult time for my parents, who now had to find a place to live and somehow provide for their children. Fortunately, Mr. and Mrs. Ivan Gerasimoff, longtime family friends who had earlier sought refuge in Hakone, were able to take us in for a few months, until the war's end. Only then were we able to return to our own house, next to the Yokohama French Consulate on the Bluff. This property had been taken over by the Japanese government some years earlier since it was located on the Bluff, which was off limits to all foreigners. I've been told that, during the war years, the Japanese military positioned an anti-aircraft artillery battery close to our house.

Contemporary writers often write about the hate and hysteria that occurred on the West Coast of the United States during WWII, and the internment of Japanese nationals and their US-born children. However, in my view, they omit the totality of that period by concentrating solely on the West Coast side of the tragedy. Some of these revisionists would make one believe that it was America that started the war in the Pacific. In fact, Japan was the aggressor, starting with its encroachment of Manchuria in the early 1930s, and then China proper and beyond, culminating in the attack on Pearl Harbor on December 7, 1941. At least some of the anti-Japanese hate, suspicion, and animosity, are understandable, in view of the Japanese militarists' brutal track record during the years preceding Pearl Harbor.

I would like to acquaint the reader of how the Japanese wartime government treated its residents, particularly those who were foreign born and many who had Japan-born children. People may not be aware of it, but there were thousands of such permanent residents living in Japan who suffered greatly during the war period. All gaijins (non-Japanese residents, regardless of whether they were born in Japan or came from abroad) were generally viewed as enemy spies and collaborators. My parents, originally from Russia, happened to migrate to Japan from China in the late 1920s. My siblings and I were all born in Japan, but unlike America (which granted citizenship to Japanese Americans born in the United States), Japan followed a discriminatory citizenship policy. Unless you were a Japanese native of pure Japanese racial stock, the doors to citizenship were generally closed to you.

After Pearl Harbor, we were under constant surveillance and harassed continuously. When all foreigners, including the French and Swiss teachers at St. Joseph's, were ordered to leave Yokohama's Bluff area, our family relocated to the Sagiyama neighborhood. The Kempeitai, the Japanese equivalent of the Gestapo, harassed us by visiting our home at all hours of the day and night, performing spot searches. I remember them even checking the kitchen pot to see what my mother was cooking for dinner.

As the tide of war turned against Japan, with constant bombings of Japanese cities, the treatment of resident aliens worsened. If someone expressed the mere thought that Japan might lose the war, that was cause to be picked up by the Kempeitai for questioning, often accompanied by beatings, and in some cases, even worse. Toward the end of the war, life in Japan deteriorated so much that people were literally starving, especially the gaijins. On May 29, 1945, we lost everything. My father suffered burns to his arm but recovered. Somehow, out of the ruins that were postwar Japan, we survived. In retrospect, I must admit that I would have preferred living in a relatively safe and well-provided US internment camp like Manzanar or Topaz, rather than under the constant police surveillance or the carpet bombings of the B-29s that were blanketing us in Yokohama, or the atomic bombs in Hiroshima and Nagasaki.

I don't have to detail the horrors and atrocities perpetrated by the Japanese militarists against non-Japanese civilians outside of Japan and in areas of their occupation (i.e., China, Korea, Philippines, etc.) to emphasize that they had a direct bearing on the atmosphere of hate and suspicion that occurred in California and along the West Coast. Those were horrific times, and when we think about the agony and suffering of the Japanese Americans, it's important to remember the plight of the subjugated people in Japan and elsewhere who suffered similar, and worse, treatment at the hands of the Japanese militarists. Those of us who were there, and especially the downed American pilots and other POWs, who survived, will never forget the truth of the Asian Holocaust in WWII.

Unlike the US government's belated apology and compensation to Japanese Americans, modern, democratic Japan has consistently shied away from any responsibility for its actions in WWII. Instead, it prefers to evade the whole subject, rewriting the history of the Pacific War at every opportunity.

My parents' wedding day, Harbin, Manchuria, October 3, 1927.

CHAPTER 2
The Lavrov Family

My family's roots go back to Imperial Russia. My father, Saveli Klementevich (son of Klement) Lavrov was born in 1898 in the rural community of Krasnoufimsk, in the Urals. My mother, Daria Fyodorovna (daughter of Fyodor) Dolya (or Dolina) was born in 1903 in the small village of Chishki in western Ukraine. My mother's family, when she was a young girl, moved to Primorye, in the Russian Far East. They went there to take advantage of resettlement benefits for farmers known as the Stolypin Agrarian Reforms. This was during the period of the early twentieth century, when, with the expansion of the Trans-Siberian Railway, migration to Siberia and the Far East increased significantly—approximately 2.8 million people between 1908 and 1913 alone.

The members of my father's family, though not wealthy, were successful landowners. Saveli, together with his father and brothers, worked on the family farm until World War I, when he left to join the Russian Imperial Army. At one time, he fought in an artillery division on the Austrian front, where he lost some of his hearing in one ear; on another occasion, he served in the cavalry. When the Bolsheviks overthrew the czar and his government, civil war erupted and Saveli joined the White Army. Under the

1928 г. дочиносеки
Японии на Пасхе
снимались

Russian Easter celebration. My parents with
Mr. and Mrs. Glinkin and Japanese neighbors in
Ichinoseki, Japan, 1928.

command of Admiral Kolchak, Supreme Leader of Russia, my father fought the communist Red Army all the way through Siberia until, finally, the Whites were forced to retreat and seek refuge in Harbin, Manchuria.

With Vladivostok also in revolutionary turmoil, and with a relative already in Harbin, my mother decided to move to Harbin, which after 1918 became the largest Russian enclave outside of Russia. As fate would have it, her and Saveli's paths crossed, and they were married there on October 9, 1927.

Harbin, located on the banks of the Sungari River in Manchuria, was established in 1898, when Russia commenced building the Chinese Eastern Railway (CER). This extension to the Trans-Siberian Railway provided a vital shortcut from Chita in Siberia to Vladivostok in the Russian Far East, and links to Dalny (Dalian) and the Russian naval base at Port Arthur. The Japanese invaded Manchuria in 1931, when the White Russian population in Harbin numbered 200,000. After Japan created their protectorate, Manchukuo, Japanese troops occupied the city in February, 1932, and proceeded to exert control over the local and foreign population. Eventually, Harbin became the center for Japan's infamous Unit 731 at Camp Refuge, which was responsible for some of the most grisly biological and germ warfare atrocities of WWII.

My parents lived in Harbin for a relatively short time before moving south to Shanghai. Harbin was saturated with White Russian refugees, and employment opportunities were limited. After failing to find a suitable job, my father decided to take Mother to Shanghai, where there were fewer White Russians and more jobs—or so he thought. Shanghai, in the era prior to World War II, was the largest international city in northeast Asia. Known as the Paris of the Orient, as well as the Pearl of the Orient, it was a thriving cosmopolitan city with, in 1930, a population of more than three million. After working for some time in Shanghai, my father heard from friends and business acquaintances who had traveled to Korea and Japan, that there were much better business opportunities there. So, still in search of a better life, my folks decided to move to Japan.

Japan, in the late 1920s and 1930s, was still transitioning from the old, traditional Japanese way of life to a more Western one. One manifestation of this change was in the clothing of the Japanese, especially for the men. They were changing their business attire from the traditional Japanese kimono to a western-style business suit. As a result, there was a huge demand (especially outside of Tokyo and other major cities) for western clothing. As most White Russians didn't speak Japanese, at least at first, and as there was limited work for them, they had to improvise their skills.

Family portrait of my parents with elder
brother Konstantin on left and my mother holding
brother Victor (II).

My brother Victor's (I) gravesite in Akita, Japan, 1934.

Fortunately, the market for "western-clothing specialists" offered a good opportunity; and many White Russians, regardless of their previous work or abilities, turned to the job of transforming the traditional Japanese into Western men and women—at least from a clothing standpoint. And this is the line of work my father chose to do.

In their early years in Japan, my parents were nomads, traveling the entire country, from Japan's southern tip to the most northern region, South Sakhalin. (South

Sakhalin is now part of Russia, but at that time it was under Japanese rule and called Karafuto.) In some towns, they owned their own clothing store; in other places, my father traded as a wholesaler of various kinds of fabrics. Konstantin, their first child, was born in northern Japan's Akita prefecture in 1929, followed by Victor (1) in 1934. Sadly, Victor died at three months from meningitis. He was buried in a Japanese cemetery in Akita. Victor (2) was born in Karafuto in 1935, and was followed by my sister Antonia in 1938, who also was born in Karafuto. Finally in 1941, I was born in Yokohama, the youngest.

As their children reached school age, Saveli and Daria had moved the family to Yokohama, the largest port city, with good foreign schools and, most importantly for my parents, a Russian Orthodox Church. They acquired a two-story property consisting of two apartments in a semi-western style next to the French consulate property, and settled down to a quieter, less hectic life. On December 7, 1941, Japan attacked Pearl Harbor in Hawaii, and everything began to change for the gaijin families in general, and our family in particular.

With spy fever already rampant in Japan, especially with the arrest on October 18, 1941, of Richard Sorge, a Soviet spy posing as a Nazi journalist in Tokyo, rumors were flying high. The commencement of hostilities only added to the doom and gloom feeling of most gaijins, especially the Americans and their allies, who were now enemy nationals. For the hapless White Russians, the realization of being stuck in wartime Japan, without a passport, was

Portrait of the Lavrov siblings, from left to right,
Tonia, Konstantin, myself and Victor, ca. 1944.

absolutely frightening. The Americans and other nationals could turn to their governments for help and, in time, be repatriated (in exchange for Japanese nationals living in the United States and elsewhere). The White Russians, on the other hand, who were literally folks without a country, had only their wits to rely on.

My parents endured the difficult war years, including the horrors of the May 29, 1945, bombing of Yokohama, when my brother Konstantin was killed, as well as the general deprivations and harassment that all gaijins suffered. After the war ended, and especially during the early postwar years, it was still difficult to survive in Japan, but somehow my parents managed. They lived in Japan almost thirty years, mostly in Yokohama. In February

1958, the family moved to Australia, where we lived for four years before immigrating to San Francisco in February 1962. My parents led a quiet life in the Bay Area, and in the midseventies relocated to Calistoga, a picturesque part of the wine country north of San Francisco. They lived there for eighteen years. Father and Mother were devout believers and members of the St. Simeon Russian Orthodox Church in Calistoga. My father loved fishing at the Russian River in Sonoma County and tending his vegetable garden, which was his pride and joy. Though my parents lived to see the disintegration of the Soviet Union, due to their advanced age, they were not able to actually witness the new Russia that was emerging and that they had spent their whole lives waiting for. Mother died in May 1995, and Father passed away in February 1997. Their final resting place is at the Serbian Cemetery in Colma, California, near San Francisco.

CHAPTER 3
Preschool Years (1946–1947)

With the end of the war, Yokohama became the hub of the US Army's occupation of Japan. Just as, General Douglas MacArthur, the Supreme Commander of the Allied Powers (SCAP), ruled over occupied Japan from his headquarters in the Daiichi Life Insurance building in Tokyo, Lt. General Robert L. Eichelberger commanded the Eighth Army's Japan-wide operations, with headquarters in the Yokohama Customs building. A large section of central Yokohama was taken over by the US military. This included the port area, where General Eichelberger's HQ stood, as well as choice business and scenic areas. The Yamashita Park/Bund section, where the New Grand Hotel—residence to General Eichelberger and his staff—was located, as well as large tracts on the Bluff, an upscale, predominately foreign residential area with beautiful homes and gardens, represented the crown jewels of the requisitioned property. In addition, other large city blocks were acquired for building housing for the officers and men of the Eighth Army; and later, housing for the wives and children that followed. Various recreational areas, including a racetrack, parks, a stadium, and an Olympic-size swimming pool, were also requisitioned. An army airstrip was constructed right in central Yokohama.

My sister, Tonia and I, with my godmother, Nonna Lapshakova.

At this time, many local residents apparently avoided the area most frequented by the GIs and sailors from nearby naval facilities. Japanese historian Takemai Eiji wrote that US troops behaved like conquerors, especially in the early months of the occupation. Some of the crimes GIs were accused of included black marketing (which was rife), petty theft, reckless driving (which caused many accidents), and being drunk and disorderly. There was also vandalism, assault, arson, murder, and many rapes. As a kid, I did not see very much of this behavior, except for all the spent condoms that littered the street. Some of the neighborhood children used to play with them, thinking they were balloons! Before long, however, censorship was instituted by General MacArthur's GHQ, and much less crime was reported in the press. Eventually, more and more of the war veterans were rotated back to the States, with new occupation troops, who had not fought in the war, shipped to Japan. These were not hardened fighting men, and they soon settled into a comfortable lifestyle in Yokohama and other cities and towns all over Japan.

In the Yokohama and Tokyo area, a number of White Russian girls married US servicemen in the years following the war. Nonna Lapshakova, my godmother, married Sgt. Clyde McCown on October 26, 1947, at Tokyo's Nikolai-do Cathedral. Our whole family attended the wedding, and my brother Victor and I had the honor of carrying the wedding icons. I was six years old at the time. It was a lovely wedding, with many White Russians and American GIs attending the wedding ceremony and, later, the reception in Yokohama. Though short in stature, Nonna was a beautiful and vivacious young lady. She spoke Japanese like a native and, when she was living in Tacoma, Washington, she had many Japanese war brides as her

The wedding of my godmother, Nonna Lapshakova, to
Sgt. Clyde McCown, Nikolai-do, Tokyo, October 26, 1947.

friends. Many years later, I met Nonna a number of times
in Seattle, and on one occasion, she took me to meet her
family in Tacoma. Nonna and Clyde had three children:
one girl, Barbara, and two boys, Nick and Andrew, plus
many grandchildren. Sadly, Barbara died around the same

time that Nonna and Clyde passed away, a few years ago. I shall always fondly remember my godmother, Nonna, and her family. (My godfather was my brother Konstantin, who perished during the bombing of Yokohama on May 29, 1945.)

Our family experience with the influx of US forces was generally positive. The GIs were very friendly to me, and always had sweets for us kids. They often would give us rides in their jeeps. We also received food and clothing in care packages from the US Army, as well as from the American Red Cross. The early years of postwar Japan were very hard on my parents, with many shortages. Still, our family was fortunate in that we had our own house to live in. In fact, immediately after we moved into our house, we had many White Russian friends and acquaintances lodging with us. This was also the period of my life when I was my mother's tail, as I would accompany her wherever she went. I would go with her to visit friends in Motomachi, Yamashita-cho, Honmoku, or the Bluff area. I remember accompanying her to numerous funerals at the Foreign Cemetery (Gaijin Bochi), which was close to where we lived, as well as to church on Sundays. Some of my most pleasant memories are the times I spent with her and an elderly woman whom we affectionately called Babushka Glinkina. She and her late husband, who had been a policeman in Imperial Russia, were our neighbors. Tragically, while riding his bicycle in the Motomachi tunnel one day, he was hit by a US Army truck and killed.

I would often follow my mother to Babushka Glinkina's

house, which was next door to our residence. Except for Babushka Glinkina, my mother and her friends were all middle-aged married women. On hot, humid summer evenings, we would meet after dinner at Babushka's outdoor gazebo. Babushka would burn pungent Japanese insect repellent to help drive the mosquitoes away. While sipping Russian kvass (a fermented beverage made from black or rye bread, with some alcohol content), the ladies would settle down to an evening of gossiping about friends and children, about shopping at the local fish market, health issues and who had recently passed away, and so forth. They especially enjoyed talking about pending marriages and often liked to play matchmaker. They talked about everything under the sun, and I was all ears! It was during these talks that I would propose marriage to all of them. You can image how they laughed—but they all accepted my proposal.

My sister Tonia (short for Antonia) and I used to play a lot with the Japanese neighborhood kids, with whom we were very close. I was known to them as Goshia. Around dinnertime, the kids would hear my parents shout, "Gosha, Gosha," to beckon me home for supper. The neighborhood kids tried to mimic my parents' Russian, but it still sounded Japanese, as Go-shi-a. Usually, we would start playing when the Japanese kids, who were already attending school, returned home from school, and keep playing until it got dark. And although we got along, we occasionally did have some fights. It was my older sister who sometimes fought with them, and I still remember

My Japanese neighborhood playmates and I.

how one little neighborhood oba-chan (grandmother) would come to our house to complain. Mother would always tell the oba-chan that it was a children's matter and that adults should not interfere. Usually, this response worked, and oba-chan went away mumbling something or other.

Another one of our neighbors owned a laundry and, at the time, most of his business was in washing GI uniforms. One day, the laundry owner's kid, who was older than me, made a deal with me. He gave me five worthless notes of

横浜税関
白いスマートなビルは港の入口にあり港湾を睥睨している

ニューグランドホテル
港にそう海岸通りにあって海外の旅行者でにぎわっている

★ NEW GRAND HOTEL.
★ THE CUSTOM HOUSE AT YOKOHAMA.

General Eichelburger's New Grand Hotel residence and Customs Building headquarters, Yokohama.

pre-war Japanese money, for my one US dollar. At that time, one dollar was worth 360 yen. Well, at about age five, I didn't know how money worked and fell for his trap. After I told my parents about this swap, they made sure I knew which had more value—worthless old yen or the mighty dollar!

During the summertime, there were many semi (locusts) humming loudly—"mim, mim, mim"—around our neighborhood, and we kids would try to capture these insects. It was quite a sport, with some kids having large collections of different semi species in little cages. Often, we would trade these semi treasures the same way we would swap our favorite Japanese manga cards.

Every afternoon, to the sound of two pieces of wood being struck together, my sister and I would join the neighborhood kids to watch "Kamishibai," a sort of pre-television, old-fashioned cardboard slide show presented from the back of a bicycle. The Kamishibai-ya were often older, former Japanese servicemen, who eked out a living selling a sticky candy to children, who would then get to watch a Japanese superhero story for about twenty minutes. These Kamishibai-ya would mesmerize the kids with their stories of heroes and villains. And these storytellers were good. They were like actors on stage. Almost all of the kids in our neighborhood, both Japanese and gaijin, would eagerly await the arrival of the Kamishibai-ya each afternoon, so we could watch the next series of their continuing sagas of heroism and glory.

A couple of blocks down from our house stood an old ice plant that was requisitioned by the US Army. While the workers were Japanese, the manager was a young GI officer. I don't remember his name or how we met, but we soon became pals, and it was from him that I started to learn some survival English. It wasn't anything formal, but simple conversational English. Up to that time, I spoke Russian at home and Japanese with the neighborhood kids. Before long, I would visit this officer almost every day, and eventually I became somewhat of a mascot to him. One morning a military truck arrived to pick up some ice, and a really big (possibly 6 feet 6 inches, 275 pounds) African-American GI stepped out of it. While the Japanese workers loaded the ice, this black GI talked to my soldier buddy. All of a sudden, this giant of a man turned, picked me up, and swung me around, high in the air. He laughed and did it a couple of times. I literally froze. In all my five years on earth, I had never seen or encountered such a being. I thought only Japanese and European gaijin inhabited the world. This panic attack had such an effect on me that for many weeks I avoided the ice plant, until my GI buddy came to our house to find out what was wrong with me. When he heard the reason I had stopped visiting him, he couldn't stop laughing!

The initial postwar years of Japan's occupation were managed by an international military administration composed of the victorious allies, including the Soviet Union. While the American forces and, to a lesser extent, the British Commonwealth forces (mainly located in the Kansai area) provided the military manpower for the occupation of Japan, the Soviet Union sent a military mission with four hundred members to Tokyo. It was led by General Derevyanko, who was its official representative to the Allied Council, headed by General MacArthur. Why was such a large Soviet mission needed, when the Soviets didn't contribute any forces to the occupation of Japan? The only answer I can come up with is that the Soviets were keen to divide the Japanese occupation along the same lines as Korea: South Japan (democratic) and North Japan (communist). Apparently, MacArthur would have nothing to do with this plan, and I think the Japanese can thank the United States for this wise decision. I remember back in 1946-47, the Soviet mission was located in one of the large office buildings in the area adjacent to the Tokyo Central Station. Notwithstanding Churchill's historic Iron Curtain speech of May 3, 1946, the USSR and the United States were still, technically, allies, and the mission would host an open house on Sundays. Many White Russians, including our family, visited the facility to view patriotic World War II films, followed by a social hour. Unfortunately for me, I always used to get a king-size headache from the smoke on the trains, as well as being in the mission's smoke-filled theater. That's when I realized I was allergic to cigarette smoke, and begged my parents not to take me to any of those functions.

Saint Joseph grade and high school, Yokohama.

YOKOHAMA GAIJIN) **George Lavrov**

CHAPTER 4
St. Joseph College—My Alma Mater

In September 1948, at age seven, I was enrolled at St. Joseph, a Catholic international boy's school administered by lay brothers of the Society of Mary (Marianist), headquartered in Rome, Italy. Established in 1901, it was the second oldest international school in Japan (the first was its next door neighbor, St. Maur's, a Catholic school for girls run by a French-based order, Sisters of the Infant Jesus). Our school was damaged during the war, but with the support and assistance of the American occupation forces, as well as the local Japanese authorities, it was able to reopen its doors soon after the war ended. St. Maur's was not so lucky, and it took some years for it to recover and the school to start running again. Meanwhile, St. Joseph temporarily became coeducational, taking in the St. Maur's girls. For some years after my enrollment at St. Joseph, there were still some high school girls studying at our school. My brother Victor was in the eighth grade at that time, and my deceased brother Konstantin had attended the school in the pre-war years. My sister Tonia attended St. Maur's elementary division. With the exception of a few, the teachers were all lay brothers, mainly French and American. During the war, the brothers had either remained in Japan (i.e., the French and Swiss brothers) or had been repatriated to the States (i.e., the American brothers), in exchange for Japanese citizens. From 1945 to 1953, this group of educators was led by Principal Aloysius Soden, a rather soft-spoken gentleman with a professional demeanor. Brother Soden, as we called him, had spent some years teaching high school classes at St. Joseph prior to the war. After Pearl Harbor, in early 1942, he enlisted in the US Navy. After graduating from the Boulder language school, he became a code breaker and translator, working with a team that was instrumental in breaking the wartime Japanese secret code. Who would have guessed that our Brother Soden was a code breaker!

St. Joseph was never a large school. At most it had a little over 450 students. When it reopened after the end of the war, it had sufficient space for the various educational facilities required, but the property needed to be upgraded and modernized. (This was accomplished in the postwar years). For example, in winter we had pot-bellied stoves in the classrooms. While they kept you warm and cozy if you were seated next to them, they weren't much help if you were far away. So in the winter, all of us students had our warm jackets on as we studied in class. Similarly, during the hot and humid summer season, there was no air-conditioning or other means for keeping the premises cool.

First grade was somewhat of a culture shock to me, as I spoke only Russian and Japanese. Fortunately, Brother Leo Kraft, who was originally from Switzerland and had spent most, if not all, of his entire teaching career in Japan at our

1st grade at Saint Joseph's, June 1949.

school, came to the rescue. Not only did he speak Japanese with me and the other Japanese speakers, he also had pictures of cats, dogs, chickens, and various other things that he used to teach us English. He would point at a cat and say "neko" (Japanese for cat). Then he would point at it again and say "cat" in English. Slowly, laboriously, with this and other similar methods, we learned the English language. It was especially hard for the native Japanese students, who had trouble pronouncing several letters, including *L* and *R*. For example, the phrase "I love apples" would be pronounced as "I rub appres." The goal for us first graders was to grasp enough English in preparation for the second grade, where we would no longer have any bilingual educational assistance. From then on, it was sink or swim. Out of the thirty-one students in my first grade class, only five or six were native English speakers. The rest were non-English speaking Europeans like myself, Euro-Asians, Japanese, and other Asians. Except for the class excursion to scenic coastal Aburatsubo and our teacher, Mrs. Murakami, I don't recall much of second grade. I do know, however, that by the time I was in the third grade, my English had improved considerably. It soon became my language of choice.

One of my earliest friends, in and out of class, was Konstantin Kashiloff, a fellow White Russian. He had been born in Morioka and spoke Japanese like the true native that he was. I recall how, in later years, he excelled in Japanese in language class. He brought to shame some native Japanese students with his perfect rendition of "Kichigai Bus" (Out of Control Bus), a story of how one bus went crazy, resulting in all kinds of accidents. Mr. Ichinose, the Japanese teacher, frequently praised Kostia (short for Konstantin), and gave him high marks for Japanese. Kashiloff left St. Joseph and Japan sometime after the tenth grade for the Soviet Union.

The Svensson brothers, Erik and George, sons of a Swedish trader and his Japanese wife, were good friends of mine for many years, until they transferred to Canadian Academy in Kobe. Another classmate that I used to play with in elementary school and became close friends with was John Martindale, the son of a British engineer expat who lived near the school, in front of an orphanage. Almost every day after school, when we were in the third and fourth grades, a group of us, including Kunio Kikuchi, Lew Higginbotham, T. Sakagami, and I. Saji, would play around his house. Often, we would spend time playing inside the tree house that John's father had built for him. Later on, as we grew, we played cowboys and Indians around the swimming pool area in Motomachi Park. I still remember how on one occasion, we tied "prisoners" to a large tree, and a senior St. Maur's girl strolling through the park saw what we were doing. She got upset and told us how cruel we were, "shooting water pistols and imprisoning poor Indians." Regardless, we played on until it got dark and we had to go home.

Another passion of mine during my elementary school years was playing Monopoly with the Pantuhin (AKA Patton) family. This White Russian family lived not far from us, on Motomachi Street, and consisted of Mrs. Pantuhin (a widow), her eldest son Victor (who graduated from St. Joseph in 1946), her daughters Valentina (SJC, 1947) and Kapa, and her youngest son, Vladimir (who was called Vova). Although Vova was some years older than me, we were pals. Tragically, his mother, while riding a train on a business trip, apparently had a heart attack and died. Eventually, the Pantuhin children made it to the States and pursued successful careers there. Vova moved to New Jersey, where he still resides with his family. During the early 1950s, television had not yet been introduced in Japan, and folks spent more time reading, playing games, and going to the movies. Listening to country and western music, the rage at the time, on FEN, the military radio station, was another pastime. Hank Williams was my number one country and western idol then, and his hit song, "Lovesick Blues," was one of my favorites.

When I reached fourth grade, I had Brother Joseph Gessler as my teacher. He was an elderly Alsatian Frenchman (born in 1879), and a strict disciplinarian from the old school. I know many of my former classmates will remember how swift he was with the bamboo stick that was always by his side. Sometimes, he would get very angry with some of the more mischievous students and charge at them with his stick. The fear of being hit drove the youngsters under their desks, and Brother Gessler would pound on the desk with the stick. As far as I recall, he never actually hurt anybody, but the sheer drama of it all was enough for many of the students. And yet, Brother Gessler was a kind old soul. After lunch, he would collect any half-eaten sandwiches from the students and have one of us take the food to a poor one-legged Japanese invalid and his family, who lived not far from the school. Brother Gessler devoted his life to teaching in Japan. He died in 1961 and is buried at the Yokohama Foreign Cemetery, together with many of his fellow educators from St. Joseph.

Brother Eulogio, a young Spanish teacher who was also the school's choirmaster, was my fifth grade teacher. I did so well in his class that, together with my friend Kashiloff, I got the opportunity to skip sixth grade. After attending summer school, I reentered school in the seventh grade.

Some of my Saint Joseph 8th grade graduates and I, June, 1955.

Because of the disruptions created by the war, as well as due to many students first attending Japanese schools before entering St. Joseph, many students at our school were much older than the average US student. Accordingly, whenever possible, students were allowed to skip grades, but only if they had good marks. I qualified because I entered school at age seven (instead of six), and my grades were good.

Junior high (seventh and eighth grades at St. Joseph) meant new classmates and new responsibilities. Also, with active hormones, we developed new interests—like the girls next door at St. Maur's. Before long, we became

SJC Chronicle co-editors, M. Uno and I.

teenagers and our lives started to change. No longer were we shooting marbles in the school yard. We were starting to become more conscious of how we looked and how we dressed. No longer was I a "mama's tail." Increasingly, I became more and more independent.

While I still studied diligently and still got good grades, except in algebra, my range of activities outside school expanded. My new friends now included Eric Ebbel, who along with his White Russian mother and grandmother, lived near the school. Ray Kimura, whose family resided near Sakuragicho Station; Wilbur Taura, son of a pharmacy owner near Yokohama Station; and M. Fujiwara were a few of my new classmates. By this time, I could also count Yuri (AKA George) Belonogoff as my close friend. He would have been my classmate in the seventh grade, but like Kashiloff and me, he had skipped a grade, going from sixth to eighth. The Belonogoff family, from Kushiro, Hokkaido, was a large one, with four sons and two daughters. Eventually all of the children would come to Yokohama for schooling at St. Joseph and St. Maur's.

In school, we all played sports. The best jocks were on the school varsity and junior varsity teams, and the rest of us participated in intramurals. I played in the soccer, softball, basketball, and Ping-Pong intramurals. In those days, we all had hobbies, and mine was stamp collecting. Brother Germaine, another Alsatian teacher, was our mentor when it came to stamps. He was an internationally recognized and respected philatelist.

On the academic side, some of the subjects I enjoyed most were English, history, geography, and drawing (with Brother Albert in elementary school). Math, especially algebra, was my Achilles' heel. My favorite English teacher was Brother Tribull, an American who also was my homeroom teacher in the eighth and ninth grades. Much of what I learned about English composition I have him to thank for. Other teachers that taught me included Brother Paul (biology), Brother Mazur (ethics), and Brother Germaine (French). Thanks to Brother Germaine's strenuous efforts at making us learn proper

French grammar and pronunciation, I can still confidently get around Paris with my St. Joseph-learned French.

Since St. Joseph was a Catholic school, religion played an important part in our school life. Catholic students studied catechism, and non-Catholics pursued studies in ethics. Since my Russian Orthodox faith and the Catholic religion were, in ancient times, one and the same, I was comfortable praying in the school chapel with the Catholic students. As for discipline at the school, it was firm and students were expected to act like gentlemen. In those days, we did not wear uniforms like the girls of St. Maur's, but nonetheless, we had to be suitably attired. Smoking and profanity were strictly forbidden, and any student caught committing these infractions was severely reprimanded.

While the students of St. Joseph came from all over the world, we all got along, regardless of race, color, or creed. We were happy to be part of our international school, which possessed a proud history dating back to 1901, and that was what was important, not our personal, ethnic, or religious backgrounds. The camaraderie that was forged during our formative years at St. Joseph was very strong, and has endured all these years. The brothers at St. Joseph laid a solid foundation that was to serve us so well in the future, as we went forward to pursue our life's ambitions. In the words of our alma mater's song, "Time may see us far and scattered, life may grow both dull and cold; still a claim to our affection, SJC shall ever hold!" And so, imbued with faith and fortitude, we departed St. Joseph and marched bravely into the new world that awaited us.

I left St. Joseph at the end of my sophomore year, when my family moved to Sydney, Australia. My brother Victor was already living there. Our friends and St. Joseph old boys, Mike Babushkin, Victor Minenko, and Paul Bellikoff, were also there. Liz Moses and her younger brother Jeffrey joined us some time later. Wedding bells were already ringing for Liz and Victor Minenko, and they would soon be wed in Sydney.

Yokohama Orthodox Church, ca. 1955.

CHAPTER 5
White Russian Community in Japan, ca. 1955

In the mid-1950s, the number of White Russians residing in Japan and the Tokyo and Yokohama area continued to shrink. The fortunate ones left Japan prior to the start of the war. The folks that stayed had to endure the tragic consequences of wartime hunger, lack of work, and various forms of harassment, as well as the horror from the sky, as General LeMay's B-29 bombers unrelentingly carpet bombed Japanese cities from north to south. In addition, many endured wartime indignities from the Kempeitai, the Japanese Gestapo. Our family, like scores of others, tried to obtain travel documents to Chile, South America, but unfortunately, we were too late. The drums of war could be heard everywhere, and almost all countries were no longer accepting immigrants from Japan, including stateless White Russians. After the war, some lucky White Russian families were able to move quickly to America and other countries. But most, including our family, got bogged down in bureaucratic red tape when they applied for visas to the United States. We waited and waited and waited, but the visas never came. The reason was that at that time, the United States had an immigration policy that allocated quotas, based on the size of different ethnic groups that had populated America a

Bishop Ireney's visit to Yokohama Orthodox Church.

long time ago. If you were British, for example, there was almost no waiting period, as the quota for Brits was very large and not fully subscribed. For Eastern Europeans, including Russians, it was much less. With the large number of Eastern European refugees seeking a new life in America, it took folks an unusually long time to receive the coveted visas. As for adult gaijins who were born in Japan or China, they were simply out of luck. With an annual Japanese and Chinese quota of only one hundred persons, they would, most likely, have to spend an eternity waiting for their number to arrive.

Still, we didn't give up hope. With faith in the future, we continued with our lives in war-ravaged postwar Japan, with its shortages and other economic woes. We were fortunate, indeed, to have the Orthodox Church in Japan, which provided us with spiritual and moral guidance and support. It was the Russian missionary Nikolai Kasatkin (1836–1912), who brought the Orthodox faith to Japan in the nineteenth century and founded the Holy Resurrection Cathedral, also known as Nikolai-do (Nikolai's house). He was the church's first archbishop and was posthumously recognized as a saint. Nikolai-do is a familiar landmark in Tokyo, and back in the 1930s, the Japanese had a tune for the bells of Nikolai-do. Today, there are Orthodox churches in all areas of Japan.

Since we lived in Yokohama, we regularly attended the local Yokohama Orthodox church, dedicated to the Protection of the Holy Virgin Mother. We traveled to Tokyo's Nikolai-do—or Saint Nicholas, as we called it— on major feast days, including Easter, when we attended midnight mass. At that time, the small Yokohama church was located on West Bluff, adjacent to a Japanese girls' high school. Eventually, the church property was sold to the school to allow it to expand. A replacement church was built near Yokohama Station, where it stands today. In the mid-1950s, our congregation numbered probably no more than three hundred parishioners, of which about 80 percent were Japanese and 20 percent were White Russians. The mass was said mostly in Japanese, with some Russian, by a local Japanese priest. George Belonogoff and I, together with our friend and mentor, Paul Uhov, were the altar boys. Actually, Paul was the senior altar boy and we assisted him. George and I attended the two-hour mass every Sunday, except in the summer, when George and his sisters would travel to Kushiro, Hokkaido, to be with their mother. She owned a retail store there. After church, we usually headed downtown for the movies or other amusement. My sister Tonia and her friends from St. Maur's, Liz Bellikoff and Vera Belonogoff (George's sister), would follow a similar schedule, with church every Sunday morning and their own entertainment plans for the afternoon.

For a number of years, my sister and I attended a Saturday Russian school at Nikolai-do, under the auspices of Bishop Iriney. It was a small school with about twenty-five students from the local White Russian community. The volunteer teachers were middle-aged White Russian ladies who taught us the Russian language and Russian history. Bishop Iriney was our religion teacher and taught us Bible history. I still remember how we would sit in his official chambers, and he would relate parables from the Old Testament. Many years later, I had an occasion to meet with the bishop in New York. By then, he was retired, but he still vividly recalled his many years in Tokyo. My schoolmates from Russian school included Alex Filatoff (now living in Sydney, Australia), George Arapoff (now in Reno, Nevada), Mike Arapoff (living with his wife in Petaluma, California), Irene Dolgoff (one of the few who still resides in Tokyo), the Von Hauffe brothers (who have

Russian School students at Nikolai-do, Tokyo, with
Bishop Iriney and parents. I am at extreme left of row 5;
my sister Tonia is at extreme right of row 4.

lived for many years in the San Francisco area), Nikita Dolmatoff (longtime resident of Sacramento), and Liz Bellikoff (now living in Las Vegas, Nevada).

To this day, I remember fondly the train ride home from Russian school with Nikita Dolmatoff on Saturdays. We used to spend a lot of time on the train, and occasionally had some interesting episodes aboard the Keihin Line. Japanese university students who rode the train were always pestering us to practice their English with them. They wanted to see how well they could communicate with native speakers! One day, Nikita and I decided to play a trick on one especially boisterous Japanese college student. In response to his persistent questions in English, we replied in a gibberish mixture of English and Russian. We noticed immediately that he was having trouble understanding what we said. When we asked him what the problem was, he thought for a moment and then pointedly replied, "I think you are talking bullshit!" We couldn't resist laughing. He was no dumb Japanese university student!

The White Russians living in Japan during the midfifties were mostly apolitical. Their primary goal at the time was to move their families to the United States, Australia, or some other country where there would be a future for their children. Everything else was secondary. Japan's economy was improving (thanks to the Korean War), but it still would take a long time before it could claim to be number one (or number two) in trade and manufacturing. Being gaijin and having lived through the difficult war years, most White Russian families did not envision a bright future for their children in Japan. The Soviets in Japan kept spreading the word about how marvelous Stalin's "workers' paradise" was, and their Red stooges among the White Russians kept urging the undecided to return to the motherland. Not many followed this dubious suggestion, and in retrospect, those that didn't should be pleased with their decision. It appears that most of the folks who returned to Soviet Russia had a hard life and would have gladly returned to Japan had they been given the opportunity. Even the few who might have been successful and happy in the Soviet Union, would lose everything by the early 1990s during President Yeltsin's economic shock therapy, when people's life savings evaporated overnight. I can share one such example with you. One young, talented White Russian was persuaded to move from Shanghai to Soviet Russia in the early 1950s. His case was not really typical, as he actually became rather successful in the arts field in Moscow. Still, by the early 1990s, his whole life savings were gone. To make ends meet, he drove a gypsy cab in Moscow, acquired for him by his friends from Shanghai days. He has since passed away, but when I met him in Moscow in 1994, he still fondly remembered his happy youth in Shanghai. Amazingly, after forty years, he had not forgotten his English. What a successful life he could have had in the West.

Before World War II and again right after, when American culture was becoming popular in Japan, the White Russians had already left their mark on the Japanese.

Nikolai-do Cathedral's Russian students. My sister Tonia and I are at extreme right of front row. George Bellikoff is kneeling.

Being an avid baseball fan in my youth, my personal hero has always been Victor Staruhin, who was known in Japan as Victor Starffin, the "blue-eyed Japanese." He was born in Nizny Tagil, Russia, in 1916, but his family moved to Asahikawa, Hokkaido, after the Russian Revolution. He was the Joe DiMaggio of Japanese professional baseball, before and after the war, and was the first pitcher in Japan to win three hundred games. According to Wikipedia, he started playing for the predecessor team of the Yomiuri Giants, and later pitched for other professional teams, including the Pacific (a Yokohama Bay Stars offshoot). He was the MVP in 1939 and 1940. In 1960, he was inducted into the Japanese baseball Hall of Fame. During WWII, with anti-gaijin spy hysteria and general paranoia raging in Japan, Starffin was interned in a Karuizawa detention camp with other gaijins. He also was forced to Japanize his name to Hiroshi Suda. Tragically, he died in 1957 at the young age of forty, in an accident involving his car and a Tokyo train. I met Staruhin once when he visited us in Yokohama. At that time, he was living in Tokyo with his second wife, who was Japanese, his mother, and his son by his previous marriage. His mother and son later moved to America.

As we continued our life in mid-1950s Japan, hoping that every new day would bring us news of the coveted US permanent residency visas, I became a teenager, and a whole new world appeared before me.

Family portrait with Earl Hayes, Jr., our American tenants' son.

CHAPTER 6
Teenager in Yokohama

On March 5, 1954, I turned thirteen and became a proud teenager. A little over a year later, in June 1955, I graduated from junior high and was ready for high school. By this time, English had become my language of choice. Except for the Russian spoken at home with my parents and Japanese with shopkeepers, tram conductors, and Japanese friends, I was speaking predominantly English. I was also a voracious reader and spent a considerable amount of time at the American Cultural Center in downtown Yokohama. It was open to the public and was a popular spot with Japanese university students, especially in winter, where they did their schoolwork in a warm and friendly environment. I also frequented the US Army Dependent Housing Library at Area 1 (Honmoku), which had a large and interesting variety of American newspapers and magazines. To get around town, my friends and I would make use of the army's shuttle bus service, which was free for authorized military personnel and their dependents. To the Japanese drivers, we were Americans and from our standpoint, we were simply following a policy of "don't ask don't tell."

At the time, the Catholic Youth Organization (CYO), which was part of the combined Protestant/Catholic

Chapel at the army's Area 2 housing area, provided many diverse activities for us teenagers. Together with the "army brats" attending St. Joseph and St. Maur's, we frequently went to those functions. I remember well the good times we had during roller skating trips to Yokosuka Naval Base, with a lot of jubilant singing and gaiety on the way back to Yokohama; the heartwarming Christmas caroling at various local housing venues; as well as the memorable Christmas dance parties at the Yokohama Colonial Officers Club, which had a full orchestra. I recall Dave Siedenburg was the master of ceremonies at one of these events. I also remember that I had just taken dancing lessons, and I must have stepped on the shoes of my date, Joy Johnson, quite a few times! We also had teen dances at Sacred Heart Cathedral on the Bluff. I think they were organized by the mothers' group at the Church for St. Joseph and St. Maur's students. Not to be outdone by the Catholic groups, we kids at Nikolai-do Russian School arranged, with Bishop Iriney's kind approval and support, our own teenage soirees at one of the social rooms at the Cathedral. We were a close bunch and had a great time, rocking and rolling. I remember Alex Filatoff, Vera Belonogoff, her younger sister Olga, Kostia Okuloff, and Andree Constantinidis, having fun at these teenage dances. Another favorite pastime for us teenagers was going to the movies, which we did often. I used to frequent the US Army's Bill Chickering Theater, until they started checking IDs. Since I didn't have a military dependent's identification, I could only get in as a guest of someone who had an ID. The great thing about the movies at Bill Chickering was that they showed the latest American films and admission was only twenty-five cents.

George Belonogoff and I would also go to Benten dori in downtown Yokohama, where we could view some of the latest American and foreign blockbusters. During the 1950s, at St. Joseph and other Catholic schools, a strict moral code prevailed. All films were reviewed and graded by an organization affiliated with the Catholic Church. Too much nudity, for example, would automatically stamp the film with an X rating, which forbade Catholics from viewing the movie. In 1956, a controversial film called *And God Created Woman* with Brigitte Bardot, was released in Japan and was immediately banned by the Catholics. The advertising for the film (which naturally was rejected by our school newspaper, *The SJC Chronicle*) showed Brigitte Bardot in her "birthday suit." It apparently did not bother Japanese moral sensibilities, as the censors approved the movie for nationwide release. At school, we were warned repeatedly not to see this movie. Well, since we were teenagers, our curiosity would not allow us to miss it. So one bright day, George Belonogoff and I proceeded to the theater to view *And God Created Woman*. We paid the admission and quietly proceeded to a side entrance, hoping that nobody spotted us coming in to view the banned film. As we opened the side door and entered the midsection of the theater, *surprise, surprise!* We came face to face with Father Zeinz, one of our teachers, who was seated at the end of a row right in front of the entrance door. He said nothing and we said nothing. (Again, it was don't ask don't tell.) As adroitly as we could, we tiptoed toward the front of the theater, as far away as possible from the good father. After the movie, we made a careful exit, avoiding anybody we knew, and swiftly made it to the street. George and I then wondered what consequences awaited us in school the following week. As luck would have it, there were no consequences. Father Zeinz never mentioned it, and we definitely had no intention of bringing up the subject.

In addition to the movies, one of my favorite activities as a teenager was to attend our school's varsity team games. St. Joseph had strong soccer and baseball teams, but its basketball team had many challenges. Our archrival across town was the US Army's military dependents' school, the Yokohama American High School, or Yo-Hi. I remember, in particular, one instance when our St. Joseph Saints basketball team played the Yo-Hi Red Devils at their gym. A large group from our school came to cheer for St. Joseph. Our junior varsity played the Yo-Hi team first, and the score was very close throughout the game. At the end, the Saints edged out the Devils by a few points, and we were all ecstatic. After the intermission, the varsity teams played, and right from the start, our blue and white Saints were trailing. The Devils were much taller and played a hard game. Our cheering section went crazy, trying to encourage our team to play harder, but to no avail. At the end, Yo-Hi had clobbered us by a wide margin. Almost as soon as the game ended, a fight erupted between some kids from Yo-Hi and our school. I don't remember all the details, such as who started it and how it ended, but a number of our senior students got into big trouble. Apparently somebody got hurt, and the school administration was very concerned about the matter.

Some months later, during the spring, our school's baseball team was playing Yo-Hi on their field. We had a Japanese student who was a fantastic pitcher, and, one by one, he struck out most of the Yo-Hi batters. It was a great victory for our Saints. At the end of the game, George Belonogoff and I, almost hoarse from the loud cheering and shouting, headed home. It was already dark, and as we walked by the dimly lit dependent housing's bowling center, we were suddenly accosted by two Filipino Yo-Hi students. One of them pulled out a switchblade. Apparently, they were upset at the Yo-Hi loss and were seeking revenge. Just as the knife-wielding dude closed in on me, my guardian angel, in the form of a military police vehicle, appeared in the nick of time. The MPs inside the vehicle must have sensed something was wrong, as they slowed down to almost a stop. Seeing the MPs, the Yo-Hi students quickly turned and walked away from us. We also left the scene immediately, walking to the house where my classmate Kashiloff lived. Why on earth we went there remains a mystery to this date. Perhaps we wanted some reinforcements, just in case.

To finance some of our extracurricular activities, many of us teenagers found part-time work, especially during summer vacation. I remember the lawns I mowed at the army's Area I Housing. It was always easy to find this work.

I would go to a dependent's house, ring the doorbell, and ask if they wanted their lawn mowed. Eight out of ten times, the answer was yes. I think ringing doorbells, at this early stage in my life, gave me the confidence to help me later, when I was in charge of sales and marketing for an international insurance and brokerage company. Teaching English was another way of making some yen, and I tutored a young Japanese boy in Kawasaki every Saturday afternoon for a few years. Our family's Japanese friends, the Yamadas, wanted their five-year-old son, Koji, to become a successful Japanese businessman, and felt that it was important to start preparing early for his English education.

Eventually, I was able to make more money getting roles as an extra in Japanese films. The Japanese movie industry produced many films in the late fifties, and often needed foreign extras. Many young White Russians joined other gaijins in these endeavors. The movies were usually filmed at studios located far from central Tokyo, and the filming required long periods of waiting. For example, for a five-minute scene, we often had to wait up to four hours until the set was finalized. Still, the pay was good, although it took a long time to receive it from the booking agent. I was cast as an extra, usually playing the role of a soldier. I was a British soldier, in shorts, in a film about the Japanese army in Burma; a Russian soldier in a movie about the Russo-Japanese war; an American GI in occupied Japan; and so on. Once, I was a cowboy in a scene in which my brother, sister, and even my father appeared. Father was a saloon

Group photo of my high school freshman class school excursion with Brother Francis Tribull, homeroom teacher.

bartender. The film was called *Hanayome Boshuchu (In Search of a Bride)*. It starred Hisaya Morishige, the famous Japanese screen and stage actor, and was directed by Yoshitaro Nomura. It was a Shochiku studio production. That particular scene depicted Morishige having a dream in which he was a cowboy at a saloon in the legendary Wild West. Another film that my brother, sister, and I appeared in was Nikkatsu studio's *Kurutta Kajitsu (Crazed Fruit)*, which was about a group of rebellious young people and their escapades in the resort towns of Kamakura and

Hayama, located about forty miles south of Tokyo. One of the stars in this film was Masumi Okada (AKA Otto Sevaldsen), an alumnus of St. Joseph, class of 1955. My siblings and I were in a cabaret scene that was filmed on location at the Blue Sky Nightclub, next door to the New Grand Hotel in Yokohama. Another movie that I played an extra in was a Japanese war film with a sort of anti-war message, called *The Burmese Harp*. You can view *Crazed Fruit* and *The Burmese Harp* on Netflix.

Once I was a teenager, I remember that both the Japanese police and the American military police started taking a keener interest in me. When I was younger, there was a Japanese cop at our koban, or neighborhood police box, who always was cordial with me. I used to greet him with a friendly "Os" (Japanese for *hi*) almost every day as I went to school. Not long after I turned thirteen, he stopped me one day and demanded I show him my gaijin toroku (alien registration) document. I couldn't believe that after all the years, he wanted to check me out. And I told him so. Perhaps he had received orders from higher up to keep an eye on the gaijins, including the teenagers. On another day, the American MPs also expressed an interest in me and one of my friends. George Belonogoff's older brother, Serge, and I decided to go see a movie downtown. Serge was wearing his usual navy pea coat, and I had my leather air force jacket on. As we were strolling toward the theater, a military police jeep rolled up, and two husky MPs hopped out in front of us. "IDs please," barked one of the military cops. Serge and I were startled by this unusual attention and explained that we weren't American GIs or sailors gone AWOL. Looking at Serge and his navy pea coat, they appeared skeptical of our explanation. When they insisted that we show our identification, we pulled out our gaijin toroku documents, which were in both Japanese and English, and which every foreigner in Japan, age twelve and over, was required to carry at all times. (The US military forces, including civilian employees and dependents, had their own identification.) They stared at our alien registration papers, which showed our nationality as stateless, and still seemed to disbelieve that we really were White Russian students. After all, we looked American, dressed as Americans, and spoke like Americans, so we must be Americans! They held us up for almost half an hour before, almost reluctantly, telling us it was okay to go.

As a stateless gaijin teenager in Yokohama, I longed to move to America and continue my life there. In fact, I remember how we teenagers would often say we came from San Francisco, when Americans asked us where we were from. We felt that we were Americans. All we needed were those coveted US visas to formalize our legal status.

Yokohama teenagers.
From left to right, Alex Bellikoff, myself, my sister Tonia and
Vera Belonogoff. Olga Belonogoff is in foreground.

CHAPTER 7
Sayonara Nippon

By the mid-1950s, my family was eager to leave Japan for a new life in America. We had applied at the Yokohama American Consulate for immigrant visas but, after a wait of many years, had no luck. So what were we to do? Did we continue waiting forever? That was our dilemma. Meanwhile, life in Japan wasn't getting any easier for my parents. Although both my brother and sister were working at the US Army's Japan Central Exchange in Ofuna, the long-term prospects for us gaijins in Japan seemed bleak. Japan played a vital role in supplying the US forces with much needed war-related material during the Korean War. As a result, Japan's trade and commerce was growing, both domestically and internationally. However, the country was still recovering from the ravages of World War II, and its main priority was to better the living conditions of its own Japanese citizens.

As our visa application to the States was getting nowhere, we had to turn to Plan B. Fortunately, Australia at that time was keen to accept more European settlers, so we decided to apply for permanent residency in Australia. Before long, my brother Victor obtained his Australian visa and headed for Sydney. Meanwhile, some friends of ours, including Paul Bellikoff and Victor Minenko, also

George Belonogoff and I exiting the
Yokohama Orthodox Church.

left for Australia. Our plan was to have Victor arrive first
in Sydney and pave the way for the rest of the family.
Sometime before our family sailed for Australia, another
good friend of ours, Mike Babushkin (who had played
on the St. Joseph varsity basketball team) and his mother
also received their Australian papers. To give Mike an
appropriate send-off and to celebrate our future lives in
Sydney, Mike and I decided to drop by a bar on Isezaki
Street in Yokohama's shopping and entertainment
district. It was early afternoon and the place was deserted,

except for the bartender and two not-so-young Japanese bar girls who were chatting in a booth. I was sixteen and, technically, too young to be in a drinking establishment. But in those days the Japanese did not generally check the identification of young gaijins. Besides, Mike was about twenty-five years old, and probably knew the bartender. Being in jovial moods, we didn't hesitate to join the ladies for a drink, and before long we were dancing with them to some tune on the jukebox. Suddenly, three young American sailors from Kamiseya Naval Communications base (located on the outskirts of Yokohama) burst into the bar, creating an immediate ruckus. While I was dancing and trying to ignore them, one of the sailors, who was very drunk, crept up to me and, without any warning, landed a right hook straight on my jaw. As I hit the floor, I saw stars. Within seconds, I was up and Mike was at my side, ready to smash the drunken sailor's face. The drunk's buddies immediately began apologizing for their inebriated buddy, and forced him to shake hands with me. I went along with the charade, somewhat reluctantly, and shook the drunk's hand. Fortunately, I didn't suffer any broken teeth or any other injury. Meanwhile, the bartender had summoned the local police, and two of their omari-san (cops) appeared in a flash. With the scuffle over, and since two of the Kamiseya sailors were forcefully hustling their drunken comrade away, Mike signaled the bartender that everything was okay. The barkeep said something to the Japanese cops, and just as quickly as they had appeared, they were gone.

About half a year later, my family was finally ready to depart for Australia. Our estimated departure date was sometime in the summer of 1957. I was happy for two reasons: we were finally leaving Japan, and I didn't have to prepare for my junior year in high school. I was looking forward to my last carefree summer vacation in Yokohama. As it turned out, we didn't leave in the summer or fall of 1957. It wasn't until February 1958 that our designated ship finally arrived and we were able to leave for Sydney. The departure delay was due to the Japanese steamship company. As there was no regular passenger steamer service from Yokohama to Sydney, our only option was to sail on a cargo ship. Unfortunately, there were not many freighters bound for Sydney either, so we ended up waiting a considerable time before our ship finally arrived. The vessel we boarded was Nippon Yusen Kaisha's (NYK) Ginyo Maru, a cargo ship with accommodations for twelve passengers. We had thought we would sail right out of Yokohama port and, if the weather was fine, be able to wave sayonara to Fuji-san (Mount Fuji). Unfortunately, NYK company policy was to load only freight in Yokohama and have all passengers embark in Kobe, a major seaport about two hundred fifty miles south of Yokohama. And so, we made rail arrangements to travel to Kobe.

As the Shinkansen, or bullet train, did not exist in 1958, we had to take an overnight train to Kobe. These trains were crowded with Japanese businessmen who smoked a lot, and the air was stifling. To be more comfortable, the businessmen normally took off their pants while they sat

Myself dressed in my favorite leather jacket.

in their seats or sauntered around the railway carriage. Underneath their street pants, the men usually wore fundoshi, the basic loincloth; and over that they wore steteko, long, loose cotton drawers, uniquely Japanese. They were akin to boxer underpants, but they extended below the knees. Removing their pants was an accepted

Australia bound aboard the *Ginyo Maru*.
My sister and I with our Japanese shipmates, February 1958.

Japanese practice on overnight trains, and the sight of half-dressed businessmen, often drinking beer and smoking, was very common. My family and I were not shocked, since we were accustomed to such practices. But I've often wondered how some American or English matrons on their first trip to Japan would react, traveling on a crowded overnight train and suddenly seeing men loosening their belts and taking off their pants!

We reached Kobe early on the morning of February

3, 1958, and that afternoon, the *Ginyo Maru* set sail on a course straight for Sydney with a full manifest of cargo, plus eight passengers, including four members of the Lavrov family. I was very happy and confidently looking forward to a new life in Australia. The passengers aboard the *Ginyo Maru* included my parents, my sister Tonia, two Canadian women in their midtwenties, a Japanese Protestant priest on a six-month sabbatical assignment to Australia, and a young Japanese au pair assigned to the Japanese diplomatic mission in Australia. The onboard accommodations were comfortable and spacious, with two bunks per cabin. I shared my room with the priest, a quiet, lean middle-aged man, and my sister bunked with the young au pair. NYK provided a purser and a doctor to look after our needs. Tasty European meals were served in the officers' dining room, and we were always joined by one or more of them, including the captain, who was most gracious. NYK stocked the parlor room with games, books, and records, and we made use of them to while away the time. We also talked and joked a lot, especially with the young Canadian women. They had spent some time touring Japan and were now heading to Australia on a working holiday. The short, bespectacled ship's doctor, who had nothing to do other than be available in case of emergencies, spent a lot of time practicing his English with us.

As we sailed toward Sydney, the sea was unbelievably calm and the voyage eventually became monotonous. One day, as we were shooting the breeze in the parlor, my sister made a bet with me that I would chicken out and not rub the au pair's back as she bathed. Well, I had often gone to the public baths in Japan and observed how the male sanske worked on the backs of (usually) elderly Japanese men and women. So without any hesitation, I accepted the challenge and, at the appropriate hour, called on the au pair. She was ready and wrapped in an oversized ship's towel as she led me to her bath. As the diminutive au pair squatted and dropped her protective towel, I started giving her back a really good rubdown—one she would never forget. She remained quiet while I rubbed her back, and before long, it was all over. I had won my bet with Tonia, who thought the game was hilarious. The au pair seemed pleased, as well. She could now tell her Japanese girlfriends the story about how a young gaijin sanske rubbed her back on the voyage. Her excited friends would giggle and wonder if there was anything more to it. And I, of course, had won the bet. Furthermore, I was now an honorary gaijin sanske. The result of the episode was a win for all!

On February 19, 1958, sixteen days from the time we sailed from Kobe, Japan, the *Ginyo Maru* steamed under the famous Sydney Harbour Bridge. Our shipboard fun and games were over. We had finally arrived down under. The vast semi-arid continent of Australia lay before us, together with a new future, with all its challenges and surprises, in a predominantly British and English-speaking land. As new Australians, how were we going to fit into this new world? I wondered. It wouldn't be long before I found out.

CHAPTER 8
Life Down Under

As the *Ginyo Maru* glided into its slip at Woolloomooloo, we could see some members of our Australian welcoming party awaiting our arrival. I saw my brother Victor together with the Satrapinsky family, at whose home Victor had been lodging, as well as our good friend Paul Bellikoff. It was an exhilarating moment for our family when we stepped off the ship and onto Australian soil. For my parents especially. Since arriving in Japan in the late 1920s, they had not traveled abroad for close to thirty years.

Once we took care of the disembarkation formalities and had our personal and household baggage loaded onto a truck, we proceeded to the residence that Victor had rented for us. It was in Marrickville, a centrally located suburb of Sydney. Along the way, while sitting with Paul Bellikoff atop the baggage in the back of the truck, I marveled at the colorful scenarios around us. Buildings and homes were painted in bright, colorful hues, and I noticed the numerous parks and abundant greenery along the way. Compared to Japan's drab postwar cities, Sydney appeared so much brighter and more cheerful. Paul's humming of popular American songs as our truck rumbled along added to the overall pleasant atmosphere.

The rented house was a brick duplex, and our immediate

Partying at Paul Bellikoff and Victor Minenko's flat.
My brother Victor is at extreme left and I'm next to him.
Paul Bellikoff is below me in center.

next door neighbors turned out to be a cheerful middle-aged couple with a teenage son and daughter. They were our first Australian mates, and we got along very well with them. After our arrival, our family quickly got organized. Victor arranged for Tonia to work as a keypunch operator in the company where he and our friend Mike Babushkin were already employed as data processing programmers. I was to apply to the local public high school to complete my education, and my father was going to see what work options were available for him. Within days, my father, our helpful consultant Mr. Satrapinsky, and I drove to the high school to meet with the headmaster regarding my enrollment. I provided him with my St. Joseph report card information, and after they received my transcripts, I was accepted. I attended the school for a week, met my fellow Aussie students (boys and girls, as the school was coeducational), as well as some of the teachers. However, after seriously considering my future, I decided I would be happier if I went to work. It wasn't due to the traditional uniforms that the kids wore, which included those round straw hats that you typically see banjo players wearing, but the very different Australian educational program, which I was not used to. Another reason was that I needed funds for various expenses. Accordingly, I decided to look for a job.

My first step in entering the corporate world in Australia was to check the classified want ads in the local newspaper, the *Sydney Morning Herald*. I had just turned seventeen and had no office working experience whatsoever, so my options were limited. I had to start at the very bottom. I applied for an office boy position at Gibbs, Bright & Co, managing agents for the Law, Union and Rock Insurance Company. Their office was located near Circular Quay, the underground station next to the ferry terminal. I was hired, replacing a young bloke who was being promoted after spending about a year as a junior office boy. It was agreed that after some on-the-job training by the recently promoted young chap, I would be on my own. Essentially, the job of the office junior was to handle the mail, deliver insurance documents to nearby insurance entities, perform all sorts of simple clerical tasks for the seniors, and be on standby to purchase the general manager's special brand of strong Canadian cigarettes, called du Maurier. So, during the next six months, as the firm's office junior, I took on the role of in-house mailman, learned my way around downtown Sydney, became familiar with various insurance documents, and most importantly, grew accustomed to dealing with the local businesspeople. This was important, as I had never worked in any kind of business capacity before. After six months, I promoted myself by resigning from Gibbs, Bright & Company. I felt that I was ready to seek a more responsible position. My tenure as office junior had come to an end.

Again, I turned to the want ads, and soon spotted a claims assistant position at the head office of Bankers and Traders Insurance Company (B&T), located on Pitt Street near Martin Square, in the very heart of Sydney's financial center. I interviewed with the management of this long-established firm, explained my circumstances, including the position I had just resigned from, and was immediately hired. I couldn't believe my luck. It seemed so easy to find employment in Sydney. Of course, it was a junior position, and the pay was nothing to brag about. Still, I was happy now that I had a clerk's position, which I interpreted as a notch higher than that of an office junior. I would work as an assistant to the senior, Michael Price, a tall, slim middle-aged bachelor, who was handling the record keeping of B&T's domestic and international claims.

From my first day at this head office position, I noticed that the pace of work was much slower than what I had encountered at my previous job. B&T's head office was located on the top floor of a tall, pencil-shaped building. About fifteen people worked there, including two in the upper penthouse addition, which barely had enough room for them. On my floor there were a number of spacious offices for the firm's directors, plus an open area for the various administrative, financial, and claims-handling employees. Except when the periodic corporate reports and statements were due, the working environment was very relaxed. My job entailed logging by hand into a massive claims register book, B&T's domestic and foreign claim figures and statistics. I also reviewed their international claim advises from Australian island areas, plus Israel. I noticed after a while that the office modus operandi was to work for about an hour or so, and then to consult with your senior or other associates. The consultations would then lead into a general discussion about almost any subject, including the local football scores. In my case, for example, if I or my senior, Mr. Price (all seniors were addressed as Mr., Mrs., or Miss) had some questions regarding any Israeli claims, I would go upstairs for a consultation visit with another new Australian, a portly middle-aged Sephardic Jew from Egypt, whose name I do not recall. He was a proud family man and enjoyed talking about his only son, his family, and the life he had led in Egypt. If the other occupant of this small cubbyhole of an office,

John Hunter, a bronzed, lanky bachelor, was at his desk, he would invariably join us, and then our consultations could literally last for hours! This latter gentleman, who was responsible for financial reporting, was an aficionado of American pop music, and continuously hummed and talked about the latest American rock and roll tunes that were currently popular in Sydney. (*Peggy Sue* was a particular favorite of his.) I remember when the tune *Battle of New Orleans* hit the radio waves in Sydney. He was so excited, he could not stop talking about it, and asked me all sorts of questions. The Aussies in general, and the youth in particular, were absolutely wild about American pop music and culture. At the time, there were also some locally produced hits, including the ditty *Tie Me Kangaroo Down Sport*, which was a particular favorite of mine.

Aside from work, life in Sydney was quiet and eventually became somewhat boring. In the late 1950s and early 1960s, there were many blue laws still in existence, which restricted work, commerce, and other amusements on Sundays. Also, on weekends, the trains ran on limited schedules, if at all, and we had a problem getting around town. Sydney is a large and spread out metropolis, and I didn't own a car. Except for some sporting activities, there wasn't much to do on Sundays. Of course, if you were a veteran, there were always the Returned Soldiers League (RSL) clubs, which did a flourishing business dispensing beer and other alcoholic beverages to their members. During my four years in Sydney, we tried to make our own entertainment as best as we could. My brother Victor joined a neighborhood jazz band, in which he played the saxophone. We also went to various musical shows and other entertainment in town. I remember one time I won a theater pass at my office for *My Fair Lady*, with dinner for two. On another occasion, I joined my brother in attending an Ella Fitzgerald concert. We also enjoyed some of the numerous Dixieland jazz sessions at various Sydney locations. The big weekend event in Sydney, as in all Aussie cities at the time, was the Saturday night town hall dance. Everybody, young or old, individually or in pairs, was welcome to attend these dances. It was a big affair, with the ladies in their newest frocks and the gentlemen in suit and tie. My brother Victor, Mike Babushkin, and I occasionally attended these dances, where, to the music of a big band, the folks would swing to Benny Goodman or Glen Miller. We would dance with the local sheilas (Australian slang for girls) to such tunes as *Waltzing Matilda*, *Pride of Erin*, and many other English, Scottish, and Irish favorites. On other occasions, our friends from Japan, Paul Bellikoff and Victor Minenko, hosted beer busts with local Aussie mates and Japanese businessmen working in Sydney. They were a lot of fun, but the mornings after usually were not!

While in Australia, I observed that the average Australian's leisure time essentially involved four favorite pastimes: drinking beer, playing sports, surfing at the beach, and betting at the races—though not necessarily in that order. That drinking beer was the number one favorite pastime is no exaggeration. The Aussies produce excellent beer, and there is a distinct beer culture in sunny, hot Australia. The locals can and do drink beer morning, noon, and night. I would often look out of my Sydney office window at 9 a.m. and notice the nearby pub was overflowing with customers, including potbellied blokes standing outside in their shorts, holding mugs full of beer. I remember the pubs in Sydney, and especially the ones that were frequented by the ANZAC (Australian New Zealand Army Corps). Mike Babushkin and I visited some of them, and we were amazed at the warmth and camaraderie of the Australian and New Zealand veterans of the two great wars, as they drowned themselves in beer and heartily sang *Rose Marie, I Love You* around the piano. No doubt they were reminiscing about the war years and the girls they had left behind. These veteran servicemen were great blokes, and it was just wonderful to spend time with them.

Next to beer, and especially with the young people, sports are what the Aussies loved most. Tennis was a big favorite, and there was an abundance of practice tennis courts almost everywhere. They played a lot of it; that's probably why they were so good at it. Football was also very popular with the Aussies, who enjoyed three categories of the sport, including Australian Rules football, rugby, and soccer. On weekends, many football tournaments were held, and that's where a lot of Australians could be found. Swimming and surfing at the local beaches was another major Australian pastime. With most of Australia's population living close to the coast, one or two of its golden sandy beaches were never far away. I used to go

Sydney departure. From left to right, Mr. Satrapinsky,
my father, Saveli, myself, Liz Moses, Jeff Moses,
Victor Minenko and my brother, Victor, February 1962.

to Bondi Beach occasionally, as it was closest to where we
lived. With a beach nearby, it didn't take long to become
a bronzed Australian. In addition to the beer and sports-
loving folks, there were also the racetrack aficionados,
usually older people. I guess they didn't play sports, so
their pastime involved betting on the dogs and ponies. I
never cared for this sport and never attended any races in
Sydney, or anywhere else for that matter.

About two and a half years after arriving in Australia, I became a proud Aussie citizen. I was fortunate—for people in my age group, there was a special law that speeded up the citizenship process. No longer would I be a stateless White Russian gaijin, as I had been in Japan. Becoming a British subject and an Australian citizen imbued a new sense of patriotism in me, especially at the pictures (Aussie slang for movies), when at the start of a feature, the image of the young Queen Elizabeth appeared on the screen to the sounds of *God Save the Queen*, and the audience immediately stood up. Becoming a real Australian, as compared to being a new Australian (a term often used to describe newly arrived immigrants), I could now share with Australians the proud feeling they had for their queen and country.

Sometime in late 1961, a miracle occurred. A letter from the US Consulate in Yokohama arrived at our house, stating that permanent resident visas, assigned to my parents and me (being under twenty-one, I qualified under my parents' quota) had been issued. I could never understand how they tracked us down after all the years, especially as we had moved a number of times in Australia before we bought our house. As I was already planning to move to Vancouver, Canada, and had the necessary travel documents ready, it wasn't a hard decision for me to simply change the destination from Canada to the United States—my life's ultimate destination. With my parents, it was a more difficult choice to make. After all, they weren't getting any younger, and with the purchase of our house, they had planned to retire in Sydney. But in the end, they agreed to move to San Francisco with us. This time, my parents and I would form the first vanguard for the States, to be followed later by my sister and brother, who would sell the house and finalize any outstanding accounts.

In early February 1962, after living for four years in the land of down under, I bid farewell to my workmates at Bankers and Traders, Sydney, and received a very kind letter of introduction to B&T's San Francisco correspondent, Balfour, Guthrie & Co., from my managing director, Mr. Molyneux. And thus, with a letter of introduction, about $100 in my pocket, and a great sense of optimism, I was ready to depart for San Francisco aboard the P&O's luxury liner, *Canberra*, and a new life in America. We would first cross the Tasman Sea to Auckland, New Zealand, and then cruise to Honolulu, Hawaii, after which we would head north to Vancouver, Canada. The final leg of our journey would have us sailing down the west coast of America, finally arriving in the city by the bay, San Francisco.

Honolulu stopover.
From left to right, myself, Giovanni, and Rene Yango,
February 1962.

CHAPTER 9
San Francisco

While the dockside crowd was still waving good-bye, the *Canberra* slowly maneuvered away from the passenger terminal berth at Circular Quay in Sydney, and then set course for New Zealand's largest city, Auckland. Traveling in class, my parents and I were starting to enjoy the voyage, when, after about two days, we reached Auckland. Auckland reminded me of Parramatta, a bustling suburb located on the western outskirts of Sydney. During our brief stopover, we were able to see the sights of the inner city, but did not have the opportunity to explore beyond New Zealand's largest metropolis. Before long, we were back aboard the liner and heading for Honolulu.

There were many young people on the *Canberra* traveling to Canada and the United States on working holidays, and I made friends with some of them. One special shipboard buddy was a stocky Italian amateur tenor, Giuseppe—or Joe, as we called him—whose uncle owned a barber shop in New York. Joe was barely five feet tall and didn't speak much English, but what a voice he had! Every night, after drinking some wine, Joe would provide us with impromptu concerts, singing at the top of his voice many of the favorite Italian arias, and receiving standing ovations from everybody around. It was fun to be around this singing barber, as we kidded him. I've always wondered how things turned out for him in his new home in New York.

It took longer to reach Hawaii than Auckland, but when we did, what a welcome sight awaited us! We were greeted by a real Hawaiian band, complete with dancing hula girls adorned with leis and hibiscus flowers. It was a wonderful moment! Later, when I was finally on American soil, I called on my friends from St. Joseph, Louis and Rene Yango, whose father was the consul general of the Philippines in Honolulu. I hadn't seen them for over four years, but to me, they hadn't changed. They were still the cheerful, fun-loving kids I'd known back in Yokohama during the late '50s. They were most gracious the whole day of my Honolulu stopover. First, we lunched at their beautiful residence. Later, they drove me all over Oahu, so I could get acquainted with the various scenic and historical places, including Punchbowl, the impressive US military cemetery. It was my first impression of Hawaii, America's fiftieth state, and I liked what I saw. No wonder some folks called it paradise.

As we headed north to Vancouver, the seas got rougher, and the *Canberra* started utilizing its stabilizers. When we reached Canada's largest West Coast metropolis, we found it to be a real jewel—a most beautiful city. I was also happy to meet one of my pen pals, Nancy Nielson, a gorgeous young, lady who showed me around the city, including Stanley Park, Chinatown, and other points of interest. She was quite genial and, being a native of

Vancouver, an exceptional tour guide. Ever since I first laid eyes on Vancouver, I've always felt a special affinity for it. (Fortunately, I would get to know it better in the future, as my business travels would frequently take me there.)

A couple of days later, and after the *Canberra* battled the somewhat stormy northwestern Pacific waters, we finally reached the Golden Gate. We arrived early in the morning to a pouring rain. It was also cold and foggy on deck, and we could not see anything of the famous San Francisco skyline. Somebody noted that it was a typical San Francisco February morning, with lots of rain and fog on the bay. Slowly, the liner sailed under the Golden Gate Bridge and finally berthed at the Matson terminal near Fisherman's Wharf. This time, our welcoming party was Mrs. Olga Belonogoff and her eldest son, Nick. Nick came prepared, having attached a trailer to his automobile to haul our personal effects.

The Belonogoff and Lavrov family ties went back many years in Japan, and when we decided to move to San Francisco, my father got in touch with Mrs. Belonogoff, a widow with six grown children. Her family kindly agreed to sponsor us to the States. As Nick drove us along the rain swept streets to the Belonogoff family residence on Eighteenth Avenue, I started forming an impression of San Francisco. It was a beautiful city with hilly districts and panoramic views of the bay and the Pacific Ocean. At the Belonogoff home, we were reunited with other members of the family, including Vera, the eldest daughter; Olga, the youngest of the siblings; Serge, my roommate for the next two weeks; and George, my schoolmate buddy from Yokohama. Another son, Gleb, was away doing his military service in the army. No sooner had we met everybody and sat down for lunch, than the telephone rang and a young woman asked for me. It was another one of my pen pals, Donna, from the Midwest, welcoming me to the States.

"George," Vera exclaimed, "you've just arrived from Australia thirty minutes ago, and girls are already calling you."

How I got my pen pals is a story in itself. About a year before leaving Japan for Australia, I answered a pen pals wanted ad in an American comic book. For a long time, I had no response, and I thought I would never hear from anyone. Then one day, the postman brought a pack of about one hundred letters addressed to me from kids (mainly girls) from the United States and Canada. Some of the letters contained photos and, in a few cases, even dollar bills! It was very interesting to read their letters, but there was no way I could respond to all of them. Almost every other week, the postman would deliver more bundles of letters to me. As a result, I got to know a number of interesting young people. With my departure from Japan, I guess the Yokohama post office realized that the gaijin "celebrity" had left the country and stopped the deliveries. I could breathe a sigh of relief!

Promptly on Monday morning, following our Friday arrival, I visited Bankers and Traders' San Francisco correspondents, Balfour, Guthrie & Co., to explore any job opportunities with them. I gave my name to the receptionist and asked to see the general manager. Soon, a tall, portly gentleman with a handlebar mustache appeared. He had dark brown hair, spoke with a British accent, and walked with a limp. Unfortunately, I've forgotten his name, but I think it was Mr. Burns. In any event, he was the senior officer at Balfour, Guthrie, and I handed him my letter of introduction, which he quickly read. He was very cordial, and we spent some time talking about Bankers and Traders, as well as my desire to find employment in San Francisco. Before long, he told me that they, indeed, had a need for an assistant in their Royal Insurance marine division. He too called the marine division's head, Clyde Nelson, and asked him to join us. After a short discussion, Mr. Nelson agreed with the general manager that I had come at an opportune time, and they offered me a position in the marine department, subject to confirmation of my immigration status. Wasting no time, early the next morning I submitted my Australian passport with its important permanent resident visa stamp to Balfour, Guthrie. The general manager checked it, found it in order, and asked me when I could start. We shook hands, and the next day I was back at Balfour, Guthrie & Co. as their new marine underwriter trainee. Not bad, I thought. Just a few days in San Francisco, and already I had a job. I guess my guardian angel was looking after me. For me, the move from Sydney to San Francisco was a seamless one; and after just a few weeks in the city, I felt totally at home. Gradually, in the weeks and months following our arrival, my parents also settled in, my father found work, and our life in San Francisco became routine.

Ultimately, 1962 turned out to be a busy year for me. I wanted to see and absorb as much as I could in my new life. Clyde Nelson, my new boss at Balfour, Guthrie's Royal Insurance marine division, was a great teacher and on-the-job mentor to me. He was the kindest and most helpful colleague in my experience, and everything I learned about marine insurance at the time was thanks to his kind and patient support. I worked almost five years under him, and I never heard him utter an unkind word about anybody or anything, except to say *darn* or *shucks* once in a while. He also recommended me to other firms when I was no longer at Balfour, Guthrie, for which I have always been most grateful. Mr. Nelson was, indeed, a gentleman and a scholar!

Soon after commencing work at Balfour, Guthrie, I decided to continue with my education. My friends and consultants in this matter were Paul Uhov and George Belonogoff. George was already studying for his degree in mechanical engineering at University of California Berkeley, and working part-time at the *San Francisco Examiner*'s classified ads department. Paul was a full-time employee at the San Francisco branch office of the major Tokyo-based Japanese trading house, Marubeni. He was also attending night classes at City College of San Francisco, where he was enrolled as a business major studying international trade management. Early on, I became interested in an international business career, so when Paul recommended the programs offered at City

College and San Francisco State University, I decided to follow his advice. I should add that I had thought of studying music with the intention of becoming an opera singer, but when I examined all the pros and cons of that career, I decided to drop the idea. As I had turned twenty-one, all I had to do to gain admission to City College was pass an entrance exam that tested English written skills, plus basic math. I passed the exam, and in early September 1962 I entered City College as a freshman. My goal, as in Paul's case, was to obtain a degree in international trade management. Since I would need a car for transportation to City College, I started taking driving lessons from a local driving school, and shortly after purchased my first automobile—a 1953 Chevrolet sedan from a used car lot on Fourth Avenue and Geary Street. I knew next to nothing about cars, but with the car salesman's strong assurance that it was in good mechanical condition, I started to drive it around the neighborhood. I felt I was making progress. I now had a job, a car, and soon would start college. The future looked bright!

And then there was a pleasant surprise. While I was reviewing some cargo insurance applications at the office one morning, a young, plump blond woman stopped by my desk and, in a cute foreign accent, asked me the way to Mr. Nelson's office. She said she was from the accounting department and needed Mr. Nelson's signature on a check. I noticed that she had typed his title as *vise* president, instead of vice president. I pointed the error to her, and we enjoyed a laugh. This was how I became acquainted

Ingrid Johansson and I, San Francisco, 1962.

with Swedish-born Ingrid Johansson, who was about my age and was in the States on a working holiday. It appears with Europeans, it is a rite of passage to take off for a year after finishing school, to travel and experience life beyond one's native boundaries. She was my first girlfriend in San Francisco, and I got to know her during the months that followed. But Ingrid had other plans. She quit Balfour, Guthrie and joined the crew of a Norwegian freighter for a long, slow boat ride to the Orient. She went to Japan and visited Kyoto, among many other scenic places. When she eventually returned to San Francisco, and prior to leaving to go home to Sweden, she called me to report on her trip to the Far East. She was absolutely ecstatic about Japan. She now lives in Stockholm, where she is close to her three children and two grandchildren.

As I reminisce, my first year in San Francisco was one of the most memorable years of my life. I felt that I had finally come home, and with the start of my college education, I knew I was on the right track. Though it would be a long journey, the train I was embarking on would carry me through to a bright and happy future. At least, that was my hope and dream!

Brother Germaine with Paul Uhov, San Francisco, ca. 1965.

CHAPTER 10
Working My Way through College

By the time I started attending City College classes in September 1962, I had a good idea of the courses I had to take. On the recommendation of my sempai, or elder classmate, Paul Uhov, I decided to concentrate on general education courses while at City and leave the rest (especially those involving my major, international trade management) for State. Also, since I had a full-time job, I didn't want to overload my schedule. As I wanted to graduate at some point, I decided to take no less than nine units per semester. Occasionally, I would scale this number down to six units if the courses were especially difficult or homework-intensive (such as accounting). I soon realized that working and studying wouldn't be easy, and would require commitment, hard work, and patience. In the end, it took me nine years to receive my BA in international trade management from San Francisco State University (SFSU). I could have graduated earlier, but the night school offered a limited range of courses that applied to my major. As a result, there was a time when I had to attend classes in the morning and work in the afternoon, in order to satisfy my major's course requirements. This approach enabled me to experience college like most college students—during the day. Between classes, I could have coffee and socialize with friends, including Maria (Masha) Mihailoff, Mary Shea, and others. I had thought taking classes in the morning would be easier on my schedule, but it was not. Attending 8 a.m. classes at City College was fine, but rushing to work in the financial district at noon every day, searching for free parking on the hills behind Chinatown, and then speed walking to the office to arrive by 1:15 p.m. was challenging. After a few semesters of day classes, I reverted back to night school. Eventually, when I transferred to State and couldn't obtain certain classes there at night, I enrolled at Golden Gate University. Its campus was conveniently located in downtown San Francisco, so I could take the courses after work and have the credits transferred to State.

And it was at San Francisco State where I studied for most of my core business subjects in the late 1960s. It was during the time when the nation's anti-Vietnam War movement was at its zenith. SFSU's radical students, augmented by outside agitators, were very vocal in their demonstrations, and they tried to shut down the campus on many occasions. Their attempts to close the university were thwarted by SFSU's courageous president, Professor S. I. Hayakawa, a Canadian-born Japanese American professor of English and semantics. Wearing his distinctive tam-o'-shanter, he would confront the radicals and, on one occasion, pulled the plug on their outside sound system. I recall sometime in 1969, I attended a meeting of a new anti-radical organization that was formed at SFSU to counter the SDS (Students for a Democratic Society). It was called SMART (Silent Majority Against Revolutionary Tactics). Their first meeting was held on campus, and just as the meeting commenced, a violent group of Marxist/Maoist anarchists (who had pretended to be part of the seated student audience) jumped up and started throwing chairs and fighting with other students. After about ten minutes of mayhem, at a given signal, they all rushed to the exit and disappeared. The first meeting of SMART had to be canceled, but it was quickly re-scheduled. When the next meeting was held at an off-campus location a few weeks later, the attendance swelled to approximately two hundred people, and security was provided by husky, able-bodied teamsters. The cowardly Marxists/Maoists were nowhere in sight. SFSU's "silent majority" was able to proceed with its meeting. As a night-school student, I wasn't greatly affected by these anti-war demonstrations. I only remember one time when I had to cross a student picket line, and even then, it was no big deal. My view, then and now, was that those radicals (regardless of any lofty arguments they might have had) were impinging on my right to get an education, and I resented them for it.

By age twenty-one, I had matured considerably and was more than ready for college. I enjoyed the general education courses, including English literature, composition writing, biology, and geology; and later, core subjects such as business law, finance, accounting and statistics—courses that would form the foundation of my business education. My college pals and I studied and worked hard, and by the end of the week, we would allow ourselves some liberty.

This meant that come Saturday night, we were ready for some entertainment. George Belonogoff and I often started the evening fun by visiting John and Zina Bulazo (nee Sitnikoff, originally from Hokkaido, Japan), with whom we had a standing invitation to watch *The Lawrence Welk Show* on television every Saturday night. After enjoying a cocktail and watching the musical program with them, we would head to a movie theater on Union Street, near Fillmore in the Marina District, to enjoy some really hilarious Japanese films. The movies were comedies about the office antics of a Japanese corporate shacho (president), with a roving eye for the ladies. The star, as I recall, was the famous Japanese actor, Hisaya Morishige. They had English subtitles, but George and I didn't need to read them, as we understood Japanese better than the translators. The subtitles were often inaccurate. We laughed so hard during these films, the theater rocked. But it was all in good fun and reminded us of our gaijin existence in Japan. After the show, we would be ready to visit some of the abundant drinking establishments lining nearby Fillmore Street. There, we would enjoy a beer and dance with some of the single babes.

On other occasions, George and I would head downtown to McAlister Street and pay a visit to the President Follies, a burlesque theater that had seen better days. It didn't have the class or elegance of New York's famous Ziegfeld Follies, but to us cash-strapped college students and the usual handful of young US Navy sailors in the audience, it was still entertaining. After all, beggars can't be choosers. Here's what we saw on stage: a small band of two or three middle-aged male musicians loudly playing their instruments, usually drums, an electric guitar, and occasionally a saxophone. A few somewhat hefty strippers in their thirties would strut around, shedding their skimpy garments to the beat of the music. Before long, at the roll of the drums, the final piece would fall and the act would be over. In those days, the ladies were never totally unclothed. They always had tiny pasties and g-strings covering their strategic areas. After the strippers, it was the comedian's turn to entertain us. "Bonjour toujour, tonight for sure," he would quip. After about ten minutes, his segment was over. Following an encore performance by the ladies, the curtain would come down. The show was over.

A favorite hangout of ours on Sunday afternoons (when we weren't preoccupied with studying for midterms or other exams) was the Hofbrau bar and restaurant on Fisherman's Wharf. It was a lively place on Sundays and featured Johan, the Singing Bavarian. He was a stout European accordion player who really livened up the place. His colorful outfit was Bavarian, complete with lederhosen and an alpine hat adorned with a feather. Johan actually was Polish, but he sure could belt out "Ein Prosit," (a German toast meaning may it do you good), the "Beer Barrel Polka", and all the other traditional German beer hall favorites. His music would draw in the tourists strolling down the street in front of the restaurant. George and I met a lot of interesting folks at the Hofbrau, including many happy young European (including German) young ladies. While enjoying our beer and to Johan's accompaniment, we would link arms and sway, singing along to the lively German music. Johan would always encourage us to perform solo numbers, and I remember often singing "Ochi Chorniye" ("Dark Eyes"), as well as other favorite Russian songs. I think our drinking buddies enjoyed hearing my songs as much as I enjoyed singing them. The Hofbrau, with its spirited oompah atmosphere and friendly people, was a fun place, and we frequented it a lot in the early 1960s.

Another favorite spot for me, and occasionally my sister as well, was the Dirty Bird, which was on Balboa Street at Fourth Avenue, just around the corner from our flat. It was our local beer joint, where one could spend hours for the price of thirty cents for one glass of draft beer. Yes, there was a bird. A large parrot resided in a cage at the Dirty Bird, and it would suddenly and unexpectedly squawk at the bar patrons. The sensation it created was eerie.

After our Saturday night out, on Sunday morning George and I would head to the San Francisco State University library, where we would hit the books for hours on end. Periodically, we would take breaks for refreshments and some conversation. During these study breaks, we were often joined by other college friends, including George Geevargis, a transplanted Assyrian; Gene Chichkanoff; Mike Izrailoff; and occasionally, Nick Koretsky. Except for me, they were all engineering students. We held these Sunday study sessions for a number of years, and all of us remember them fondly to this day.

September 5, 1967, turned out to be my lucky day, when one of my cherished dreams came true. Within six months of my arrival in San Francisco, I had submitted my US citizenship application papers in San Francisco, and exactly five years later, on September 5, 1967, I became a proud American. Having pledged allegiance to the United States, and flushed with a new sense of patriotism, I was ready to defend America from all enemies, domestic as well as foreign. I also exchanged my Australian passport for an American one, which I believed would serve me well in the future.

While I pursued my college studies, I was also ambitious. After about five years of working in the marine division of Royal Insurance, which had earlier split off from its managing agents, Balfour, Guthrie, I was ready for new challenges. I decided to move to the Home Insurance Company's San Francisco marine department, where I joined the team of veteran marine insurance managers, Jim Pettipas and John Sweeney. There, I handled yacht and inland marine floater insurance underwriting. I enjoyed working at the Home, and was able to add some more marine insurance lines to my reservoir of insurance experience. But after about a year and a half there, I resigned and moved to the East Asiatic Company, a shipping company headquartered in Copenhagen, Denmark. My job there was claims agent in connection with their cargo and other property and liability exposures. I replaced a gentleman named Serge Komov, a longtime Russian-American resident of San Francisco, who was retiring. Serge and I got on very well during the few weeks we worked together, and he quickly and efficiently taught me the ropes of their claims handling operation. I enjoyed working for this shipping company, dealing with their marine surveyors, maritime lawyers, and other business associates. Unfortunately, I had to resign after a year and a half, when I was transferred to their new San Francisco Pier 80 terminal operations. My new responsibilities would have required me to handle the claims, as well as to engage in shipping operations work, such as meeting arriving vessels, not only in the Bay Area, but in Sacramento and Stockton at various hours of day and night. I would have had to drop out of college to take on the new responsibilities. Bottom line, I decided it was not in my best interests to leave college.

After I resigned from East Asiatic, I immediately applied for a marine underwriter position at the Aetna Insurance Company in San Francisco. The position was, specifically, for an ocean marine underwriter reporting to the ocean marine director, Tom McGhee. A number of qualified people had applied for the position, but fortunately for me, I was apparently the main contender, and I was hired by the senior director. Not only did I have about five years of cargo and hull insurance underwriting experience from the Royal, but I also had a background in yacht and inland marine insurance, which I had acquired from Home. In addition, my experience dealing with cargo claims was useful. And the recommendation from my former boss at Royal, Mr. Nelson, was another feather in my hat. Because

Tania and I when we first started dating, Yosemite, March 7, 1965.

the job involved handling a large volume of yacht business, plus a smaller book of cargo and hull business, it was a good fit for me. I enjoyed working at the Little Aetna, as the company was affectionately called, and left five years later only because the company was reorganizing, and I received that proverbial offer I could not refuse from Johnson & Higgins, the second largest international insurance broker in the world.

During these college years, I occasionally would take

out a friend on a date, and sometimes double date with my buddy, George (especially if the girls knew each other and were friends). But on one fateful day, sometime in early 1965, I went by myself to the Russian Center, San Francisco's home for the Russian-American community, where a dance was being held. In the sixties, the Russian Center was buzzing with activity and the weekend dances— or balls, as they were called—were very popular. I knew most of the young people that attended these events and I figured I would stop by for a little while and check the action. While speaking to some friends, I noticed a new girl that I had never seen before at the Center. I asked her for a dance.

Her name was Tatiana Izmailkoff, and she had just recently immigrated to the States from Santiago, Chile. She had been born in Czechoslovakia during World War II to Russian parents; and her family had moved to South America, via Austria, some years after the war. She was a beautiful blond with a bubbly personality, and spoke Russian and Spanish. As I got interested in her, we started dating; and after a courtship of about two years, we decided to tie the knot. We were married on March 5, 1967, which was also my birthday (I had turned twenty-six), at the Holy Trinity Cathedral on Green Street in San Francisco. Shortly after, we moved into a small apartment in the Richmond District, close to the Russian churches, delis, and other establishments. We lived there for about six years, before we acquired our first home in nearby Tiburon, Marin County.

Our wedding day, San Francisco, March 5, 1967.

On June 5, 1968, while the hippies were celebrating their Summer of Love in San Francisco, my life took a big leap forward. With a roar and a cry, our first son, Alexander, entered this world on that day at 6:55 a.m., weighing seven pounds and fourteen ounces, and measuring nineteen and a half inches long. (Tragically, Bobby Kennedy was assassinated on the same day. I will never forget it, as I happened to be sitting in the waiting room of the French Hospital maternity ward, when the TV announced the sad news in the middle of the night.) By this time, my college education was on track, I had a job I liked, and I had just acquired a brand new Duster, a two-door sedan. But most importantly, I now had my family, which was most dear to me. Yes, my responsibilities had increased, but I wasn't overly concerned. I was confident that my personal life and business career were on track, and I pressed on.

CHAPTER 11
Opportunity Knocks—
My First International Assignment

On June 3, 1971, I finally received my Bachelors degree in international trade management from San Francisco State University, becoming the first member of the Lavrov family to graduate from college. It was exhilarating, and I felt good at my success. But the euphoria didn't last long and life continued as before. Now that I had a college degree added to my resume, I felt it was time to start actively looking for an international position. My ultimate goal was to transfer overseas and live the life of an expat for an extended period of time. At one time, I thought a diplomatic career would be worth pursuing and I sent in my application for the periodic entrance exam that the State Department conducted in our area. But when I took the test, I flunked it. After some reflection, I realized that it was my fault that I had not adequately prepared for it. Had I obtained the necessary study guides and worked with them, I think it would have made a difference. However, I decided not to try a second time but continued to explore other international career opportunities. Meanwhile, I kept busy with my work at Little Aetna's Marine Department.

Tania gave birth to our second son, Nicholas, on August 22, 1972, and we became a family of four. He was born at San Francisco's St. Mary's Hospital at 8:50 p.m.

with an angelic smile on his face, weighing eight pounds and measuring twenty inches long.

By the early 1970s, I developed close business relations with a select group of insurance brokers and agents. They produced the business and referred it to me, so I could do the necessary underwriting. Included in this group were a number of marine insurance brokers from Johnson & Higgins (J&H). They visited me frequently in connection with various hull insurance placements, and occasionally we would have lunch. During these informal lunches, we often chatted about insurance market trends, personnel changes at the various insurance companies and brokerage houses, and other matters of interest. I don't recall when, but at one of these sessions, I must have mentioned to Chet Ames, one of the J&H marine department brokers, of my longtime interest in pursuing an international career. Not long after that, Chet called on me at my office and brought up the subject of international job opportunities. We discussed the subject for a short time, and he proposed that, with my international background, foreign language ability, and experience in the insurance industry, I should consider an international career with J&H. Now that was music to my ears. I was certainly interested, but I didn't really think anything would materialize. After all, I often talked to friends in the industry about career opportunities, but nothing interesting ever came of it. On this occasion, however, I was wrong.

Shortly after that meeting with Chet, his associate at J&H, David Olsen (who would later become J&H's

CEO) came by my office, and he also picked up on the subject. As the next step, he helped arrange a meeting for me with senior J&H management, who informed me that J&H had decided to hire me for a position in one of their overseas offices. Apparently, some of the marine department representatives who knew and worked with me had strongly recommended me. I accepted their offer, with pleasure, thanking everybody for their confidence and trust in me. This wonderful opportunity was the opening I needed to jump-start my international career, and the timing couldn't have been better. Little Aetna was in the midst of merging its marine operations with another insurance company. We mutually agreed that I would not continue in their new organization, but would move to J&H in January. With this strategic career move, I commenced my life's journey into the world of international insurance business.

On January 1, 1974, I joined the ranks of J&H as a management trainee. At that time, J&H trained its overseas-destined employees for six months in-house prior to shipping them out. The objective was to instill in them the insurance brokerage expertise and professionalism for which J&H was world renowned. In my case, my training would be in San Francisco, and I would spend time in each of the departments of J&H. My first four weeks of orientation and training was with the property department. This unit was responsible for some of J&H's largest property accounts. I spent time with the individual account executives, watching how they handled the daily routine of servicing their accounts, developing competitive rates and coverages, and making presentations to their clients. After four weeks with the property department, I moved to the casualty department and followed a similar routine there. All the time, I was reviewing a lot of policy forms and endorsements, as well as asking many, many questions. In fact, at the end of my training with each department, my trainer's final comment was always, "Do you have any questions?"

One unit that I especially enjoyed training with was called property loss control (PLC). This department's responsibility was to assist clients with loss prevention. The senior managers in this unit were called PLC engineers, and actually had engineering degrees. I was taught how to sketch simple property layout maps, as well as to mark the necessary technical data. For example, in the case of a factory, the map would show surrounding exposures, the types of building construction, whether the facility had a sprinkler system, the number of fire extinguishers, and so forth. I enjoyed learning these technical details, not realizing how important this training would be for me in the future. After two weeks with PLC, I went on to the marine cargo and marine hull divisions, where I spent a number of weeks with my marine department friends and associates. I was already a marine underwriter, so my orientation there was focused on J&H's marine clients, special marine forms, J&H's marine claims-handling operations, and related activities. At the time, J&H San Francisco had a significant chunk of large West Coast-based cargo and hull accounts. Among them were some of the leading shipping companies of the world. Before long, this training period was over and management had to decide what to do with me. The plan, as agreed earlier, was for me to be transferred overseas as a member of J&H International, which was headquartered in New York. While I was in training, there was talk about a possible slot for me in Singapore, but for some reason, that did not work out.

J&H San Francisco had a small international unit of its own, headed by Don Bullard, an executive with extensive international insurance experience. He agreed to take me on his staff, until an overseas posting opened up for me. I was assigned to work with John Noden, assistant vice president. John was originally from Minnesota, an ex-marine in his thirties, with a background in servicing international accounts. I got along well with John and enjoyed working with him. He taught me the drill, so to speak, on how to coordinate and place both home and foreign insurance coverages. This involved coordinating the US insurance requirements for a corporation with the requirement of placing local overseas coverages that met local legal and service requirements. He also introduced me to all of the San Francisco-based underwriters with whom we dealt internationally—AIG, AFIA, Continental, and many more. There was also a charming lady account executive, Betty Cullen, with whom I worked, and who provided me with additional insight into the handling of international accounts. With their support, I was able to start servicing my own international accounts in a relatively short time.

Gradually, I shed my persona of a marine underwriter and emerged as an international insurance broker. After the initial training with John and Betty, my job at J&H International San Francisco was to provide full international insurance services to corporate clients (many located in Silicon Valley) that were assigned to me. No more would I be dealing with marine business only. Now, my focus was on companies based in Northern California with plants and machinery overseas. In view of my Japanese background and my ability to converse fluently in Japanese, I also started assisting other account executives in the solicitation of Japanese accounts. I read and reviewed all of the available material on J&H's international operations, so as to familiarize myself with them. By then, I was corresponding with J&H overseas offices and correspondents. In those days, it helped if one was a good letter writer, especially in dealing with overseas personnel, who tended to understand written English better than spoken English. It was all very exciting, and I was glad that I would soon be a participant in the international business environment as an overseas-based insurance broker. Meanwhile, there was quite a bit of activity in our New York international department, with some of our top international executives visiting San Francisco to interview me and work on finding me an overseas slot. But there was still no definite news on my transfer. When would my first foreign assignment become available?

Finally, I was informed that one of our Tokyo-based expats was returning to New York, and that I would be replacing him. Eureka! That was my lucky day! At last, I was no longer in limbo. I knew working in Japan would not be easy, but I was confident that I could and would meet the challenge. I was very motivated to return to the Land of the Rising Sun and do my best, so as not to let down my friends and associates, who had so much faith in me. I quickly started to make preparations for our relocation to Japan. From a living and cultural standpoint, Japan would not pose any problems or difficulties for me. I had been born and raised in Japan, spoke the language, and still had many friends in the Tokyo and Yokohama area. As for the rest of my family, I knew our sons (at the time Alex was seven and Nick was three) would have no problem adjusting to the excellent international schools in Tokyo. For my wife, Tania, it would be a culture shock at first, but I was confident that she would adapt, especially once she made friends. Her challenge would be to improve her English-language capabilities and pick up the necessary survival Japanese. After all, Tokyo was a major cosmopolitan center, with expats and their families from all over the world residing there. It also provided a variety of interesting social, cultural, and recreational activities for all.

My job was going to be interesting, and I looked forward to introducing my family to Japan and the Japanese people. Just as Japan had made an impact on me, it would also influence my family after they spent some years there. Living in Japan in the 1970s should be a lot different from my earlier days in Yokohama, I thought. For one thing, it would be a lot more comfortable than those miserable postwar days when all of us, gaijins as well as the Japanese, were struggling under very difficult living conditions.

CHAPTER 12
Japan Revisited

In July 1975, my family and I arrived at the old and crowded Tokyo International Airport, or Haneda, as it was commonly called. (The much delayed new international airport at Narita would open in 1978.) It had been a long and tiring flight from San Francisco, and as we exited from the restricted inner section into the lobby area, it seemed like half of Tokyo's residents were waiting to greet friends or relatives. Tania and the kids had never seen so many Japanese before, and were somewhat aghast at the frenzy of the large crowd. My new boss, Hal Reynolds, and his wife, Karen, were to meet us at the airport, but we could not see them or any other foreigners among the sea of Japanese faces. Finally, Karen spotted us, and after brief greetings, we hurried to their car for the short ride to the hotel.

After passing the industrial area adjacent to the shuto, or expressway, we soon arrived at the sprawling New Otani hotel complex in central Tokyo. Entering the lobby, we noticed a large Chinese delegation, with all the men dressed in identical Mao jackets. It appeared the hotel was hosting some regional conference. J&H Tokyo had made the reservations for us, and we were given the keys to a two-room suite in the tower section of the hotel. By western standards, it was small, but it was attractively furnished,

Alex and Nicky, aboard the Soviet m/v *Baikal*,
steaming to Hong Kong, December 1975.

with an ikebana flower arrangement and large picture windows providing panoramic views of the city. As tired as we were, we could not fall asleep, so we turned on the tiny thirteen-inch TV to watch English-language broadcasts from a local cable channel. The next day, I was going to the office to meet J&H Tokyo's general manager and staff, and to complete any required paperwork. Tania and the kids would have the whole day to explore Tokyo.

I awoke quite early the next morning and started preparing for my big first day at the new office. I knew the office was about a ten-minute drive from the hotel, and I debated whether I should catch the nearby Ginza Line subway or walk. It was about 8:30 a.m., already somewhat hot and muggy, and the office would be open at nine. I decided there was no point in getting there early, so I opted for the walk and started hiking along the broad Aoyama-Dori Boulevard. I had never spent much time in Tokyo when I was growing up, so I really didn't know the city and its surrounding areas very well. Plus, as my first walk to the office would show, everything was new and modern. Between when I left Japan in 1958 and my return to Tokyo in 1975, Japan received a dramatic face-lift. Tokyo, indeed, could now lay claim to being not only Japan's capital, but also the business center of Asia. As I had spent a lot of time on the plane the day before and was suffering some jet lag, the relaxing walk cleared my head. After stopping for directions from a local passerby, I approached Aoyama 1-chome, the neighborhood where our office was located. I was excited and looking forward to my meeting with Hal Reynolds, a former US Navy officer and a longtime J&H International expat. He was the vice president and head of J&H Tokyo. After about thirty minutes, I reached the multistoried building where J&H was located. When I took a moment to check the tenant listing in the small lobby area, I noticed that nearly all of its tenants appeared to be foreign corporations. Once inside the J&H office, I was greeted by Miss Saito, a slim, middle-aged Japanese woman, who was Mr. Reynolds's secretary. Upon seeing me, she jumped up from her desk and warmly said,

"Welcome back to Japan, Mr. Lavrov!" She then led me straight into the general manager's office.

Hal Reynolds managed J&H operations in Japan, and was also responsible for Taiwan, Hong Kong, and South Korea. He produced and handled some Japan-based accounts, including the prestigious Tokyo American Club, whose membership included American and foreign expatriates, as well as wealthy Japanese corporate and industrial movers and shakers. With his extensive regional travel and busy Japan operations, Hal's inbox was always full. After officially welcoming me to J&H Tokyo, he announced that my title at J&H Tokyo would be assistant vice president. I thanked him for the good news and proceeded to give him a quick summary of my marine underwriting experience, and the orientation and training that I had received at J&H San Francisco. He briefed me on J&H Tokyo's plans and objectives and the role I would play in them. He emphasized J&H's professional client service, as well as the need to develop new business from the ranks of major American and other foreign companies doing business in Japan. Bottom line, he stressed, was that as with any profit center, it was produce or perish—a concept that I would hear more and more in my insurance brokerage career.

After our meeting, Hal introduced me to the other senior staff members, including Peter Skov, a former government agency employee, now working on a new career in the international insurance field. Peter handled Taiwanese businesses. Hal also introduced me to the

Alex, Nicky and I in front of Nikolai-do Cathedral in Tokyo.

senior Japanese national, Tommy Kawamura, assistant vice president, who spoke excellent English and handled some of J&H Tokyo's largest Japanese American joint-venture industrial accounts. He was a resident of Yokohama and learned English when he worked for the US Army. I met other key senior members of the J&H Tokyo team, including Messrs. Matsuzawa, Morohashi, Hoshine, and Hamada. They all spoke English, to varying degrees, with Mr. Hamada, the marine manager, probably speaking it the best. (All of them would later relocate to the United States as business development officers.)

Hal and I discussed how best I could contribute to the success of the local operation. He suggested that, because of my marine background, I start by servicing cargo, transportation, and other marine-oriented accounts, including shipping companies, inland marine storage facilities, and air and sea forwarders. Later, when I became accustomed to Japanese insurance programs, insurance markets, and local business practices, I would expand into manufacturing accounts, including pharmaceuticals, chemicals, cosmetics, and other industries.

During the first few weeks in the Tokyo office, my flexible schedule allowed me to search for suitable quarters for our family, as well as getting our oldest son enrolled in the second grade. The rest of the time, I reviewed the files and accounts that I was assigned to familiarize myself with their history, and to discuss any questions with the account executives who had handled them in the past. I was also preparing to be introduced to the key personnel from the foreign and Japanese insurance companies with whom we did business. A welcome cocktail party in my honor was scheduled at the Reynolds' home in Roppongi, when Hal would officially introduce me to all of the senior foreign and Japanese underwriters.

As it turned out, it was a routine matter to enroll my son in the American School in Japan (ASIJ), located on the outskirts of Tokyo. It was another matter to find suitable family accommodations that would not bankrupt J&H. The rental cost for an apartment leased to foreigners in Tokyo often appeared like the semi-annual or annual rent, when actually it was the monthly rent. Many expats simply could not believe their ears at first. Of course, there were less expensive rentals, but they generally were not comfortable or spacious. Utilizing the services of a few rental agencies that specialized in foreign rentals, we searched and searched for a suitable apartment, but to no avail. We were working within the limits of J&H's housing budget, and it wasn't easy to find what we wanted in Tokyo, where the sky was literally the limit on housing costs. With the hotel expense meter running, we had to find a place quickly.

One day, my new associate, Peter, came to our rescue. He had heard from friends that a two-bedroom apartment had just been vacated at Azabu Towers, next door to the Tokyo American Club and right behind the USSR embassy. The Azabu Towers was a large high-rise apartment complex with two towers. Most of the tenants were Americans and Europeans. It was centrally located in Azabudai, next to Roppongi, the entertainment district, had good transportation connections, and was the hub of expat activities. Peter drove us to the Towers, and although

Visiting my brother Konstantin's gravesite at the
Yokohama Foreign Cemetery, together with the Bulazo family.

the vacant apartment was very nice, it was rather small.
In view of our situation, however, we decided to take it,
with the condition that when a similar three-bedroom
apartment became available, we would move into it.
(That occurred about a year later.) Fortunately, we were
able to make the hotel to apartment move quickly, as
our household goods were already in Tokyo. We settled
into our new apartment and joined the prestigious Tokyo
American Club. That enabled us to make new friends and

enjoy various social and sporting activities. Alex was ready to start second grade, and Nicky would enter a playgroup at the American Club a little later.

Residing at the Azabu Towers behind the walled USSR embassy compound was a little like living in the shadow of the KGB. The mid to late '70s were the height of the Cold War, and the political climate surrounding the embassy was tense. Fanatic right-wing Japanese radicals were an almost daily occurrence in front of the embassy. The ear-splitting racket they created with their blaring loudspeakers permeated the entire neighborhood. How the local Japanese citizens living in the area put up with these noisy demonstrators is beyond me. These wannabe soldiers of the defunct Imperial Japanese Army wore black military-style uniforms and rode in black WWII era sound trucks. You could see them all over central Tokyo, including the Ginza near Yurakucho Railway Station. Screaming in Japanese and broken Russian, they demanded the return of four small islands of the Kuriles chain, located near the Japanese northern island of Hokkaido. The USSR had reclaimed the islands during the last days of World War II.

It wasn't the rowdy demonstrations that kept the embassy employees hunkered down behind the walls of their embassy compound, though. They had another reason, which we noticed almost every day as we scurried in and out of our apartment complex. When Tania and I walked out of Azabu Towers and down a small alley leading to the nearby Juban Shopping Center, we often passed Soviet employees returning to the embassy with their groceries. We would nod or say hello to them, but it was like two ships passing each other on a dark and foggy night. They avoided any eye contact, nor would they speak to us. I remember one especially unfortunate incident, involving Vera, an elderly White Russian lady from Kamakura who occasionally babysat for us. She decided to take little Nicky to play with the Soviet children at a Japanese playground near the embassy compound. She thought it would be nice for him to play with Russian-speaking children. But it was not to be! As soon as she and Nicky appeared at the playground, mothers grabbed their children and scattered in all directions. They apparently had been warned not to fraternize with anybody outside the embassy, especially Americans and White Russians. What were they so terrified of? It wasn't really hard to figure it out. It was the Sword and the Shield of the Communist Party, the KGB, that kept a tight leash on them, and whom they most feared. Some of these political commissars resided in an apartment building next door to the embassy, and they were not afraid of interacting with anybody. I wondered when these "neighbors" would seek to make their acquaintance with me. In fact, it wasn't long before I heard from one of their representatives.

One morning, out of the blue, I received a phone call at my office. I answered with my usual, businesslike, "Hello, this is George Lavrov speaking." The mysterious caller replied, "This is Yuri ... from the Soviet Embassy. Shall we speak in Russian or English?" "English," I blurted. He continued, saying they had received a letter from Russia

Cecil Baclay, Andy Apanay and I horsing about at the
annual SJC alumni dinner-dance in Tokyo.

intended for my wife. Could I stop by the embassy to pick
it up? "No," I replied. "I am very busy. Why don't you have
one of your messengers drop it off at the front desk of
the Azabu Towers?" Yuri replied, sounding flustered, that
I was not being very cooperative. And that was how the
conversation ended. When I arrived home that evening, a
letter from Russia was in our mailbox. When I told Tania
that our next door neighbors were reading her mail, she
wasn't shocked. She simply said, "Let them waste their
time." After that, all of her letters from a relative in Russia
arrived directly to her without any detours. But Yuri's
interest in me wasn't quite over.

One evening after work, as I was walking along the

main street near the embassy, he sidled up to me and tried to initiate a conversation. "You're Russian, aren't you?" was his opening line in English. I turned my head in his direction, told him no, and continued walking. He got the message and fell back as I quickened my pace. But he was a persistent fellow, and I often noticed him hanging around, sometimes with a little leashed dog, in front of the commissars' apartment building, which I had to pass every day on my way to and from my apartment complex. But I had no intention of developing any "business" with the notorious KGB, and at some point Yuri decided to quit. Perhaps it finally dawned on him and his associates that our sympathies lay with the hapless, muzzled embassy workers that we saw daily trudging up the hill with their plastic shopping bags; and that we wanted nothing to do with their oppressors, the feared KGB. (I was already back in San Francisco when the USSR self-destructed, but I learned that the dreaded red symbol of the Communist state, the Soviet flag that had flown atop the Tokyo embassy, was replaced on December 28, 1991, with the traditional white, blue, and red flag of a free and democratic Russia.)

CHAPTER 13
Life of an Expat in Japan, Part I

As an American insurance broker in Tokyo, my job was to take care of our corporate clients' insurance and employee benefits needs in Japan. Simply put, we represented the clients, not the insurance company. While brokers can also be licensed as insurance agents, agents cannot be brokers. Agents essentially are an extension of the insurance companies. In fact, during my time in Japan, brokers were not allowed to operate legally in Japan, so technically, we were all agents of the insurance companies with whom we worked. From a practical standpoint, however, we provided the kind of specialized insurance services that our clients were accustomed to and expected to receive from us in Japan. With my past insurance underwriter background, I realized I had to retool myself if I wanted to become a successful insurance broker. I had to stop thinking as an underwriter and start putting myself in the client's shoes. What were the client's specific needs and how could I tailor the right insurance program for him, I had to ask myself. This became my top priority while I worked at J&H Tokyo. Thanks to Hal's supportive efforts in steering me in the right direction, within a few months I was able to start working on new business opportunities. By the end of six months, I had fully adjusted to living in Japan

Receiving a sales award at a Tokyo
underwriters' presentation ceremony.

(there was no culture shock for me), made the necessary
business contacts, familiarized myself with the Japanese
insurance markets, and most importantly, solidified my
interpersonal relationship with my colleagues at the office.

I also became an informal English teacher to my
Japanese colleagues, who without realizing it, helped me
with my Japanese business vocabulary. (My Japanese was
fluent, but it was strictly elementary school Japanese.)
To assist my colleagues with their English, I always spoke
English at the office. Before long, they started using some
of the same English terms and expressions I used. For
example, when they left the office, they started saying,
"See you later," instead of their usual Japanese expression.

In addition to speaking English with them, I would edit, or rewrite when necessary, their English letters or reports. By working with them daily and listening to their Japanese conversations with colleagues or clients, I was able to expand my conversational ability in Japanese considerably, to the level of the local salarymen (Japanese corporate employees) and the OLs (local slang for female office assistants). With time, my spoken Japanese got better and better. I was starting to impress Japanese clients and underwriters alike with my fluency, and this earned me brownie points.

Adjusting to our new life in Japan was harder on my family. For Tania, who had grown up in Santiago, Chile, and was a fluent Spanish speaker, Japan was a very different foreign environment. Still, she was determined to make a go of it, grasped survival Japanese rather quickly, and soon made friends with some of the American, Japanese, and Hispanic ladies at the American Club. Before long, we were attending parties and receptions at numerous embassies and private homes. On Sundays, we regularly attended services at Nikolai-do Cathedral in Ochanomizu, where we made additional new friends and reconnected with some old ones. After Alex attended the American School in Japan for two years, we decided to transfer him to St. Mary's International school in the Setagaya area, where he entered the fourth grade. This international Catholic boy's school was administered by French-Canadian brothers and had over nine hundred students, representing many countries in the world. Alex joined the school band, as well as the Boy Scout troop, and before long he was earning all sorts of merit badges. Transferring him was a good decision, we felt, as he appeared to be happier and doing better academically at the new school. After "graduating" from the Tokyo American Club's playgroup, Nicky went on to Sacred Heart International School for two years, where he attended preschool and kindergarten classes. Then he, too, entered St. Mary's. In support of the school, Tania joined the PTA, which was called the St. Mary's Mothers' Club, where she made more friends and actively worked on the annual fundraisers, picnics, and other related activities.

While living in Tokyo, I also had a life outside of the office. I reconnected with some of my former classmates at St. Joseph, and became actively involved with the school's alumni group. Its main project was the annual gala dinner-dance, which was held at a posh Tokyo hotel and attended by a large crowd of SJC alumni and their friends. Among the loyal, energetic alumni were Francis de Britto, Andy Apanay, Cecil Baclay, Rudy Fachtman, and Joe Gordo, just to mention a few. While living in the Big Mikan (big tangerine), as Tokyo was affectionately called by some of the expats, Tania and I also had many opportunities to attend concerts by world-famous musicians and orchestras, and all kinds of expositions, trade shows, and other interesting activities. We especially enjoyed the first class musical ensembles that visited Tokyo. For example, we attended a presentation of *Die Fledermaus* that was performed by a Vienna-based group; a fantastic Gypsy troupe from the

Soviet Union, whose name I don't recall; and the Red Army Men's Choir. The performance was superb—and this was one concert we wouldn't have seen back in the States during the Cold War years.

While living in Japan, we also traveled, both inside and outside of Japan. One winter Tania had a fabulous holiday with the ladies group of the American Club, traveling to Sapporo, Hokkaido, for the annual world-famous snow festival. Toward the end of December 1975, to give myself

Group picture with J&H Tokyo employees
during a company outing to Atami.

and the family a New Year's break, we decided to go on a ten-day cruise to the British colony of Hong Kong. Philip Gsell's (my former classmate) travel agency, Toppan Travel, booked us on the Soviet liner *Baikal*, a 5235-ton, 262 passenger ship that usually plied the Nahodka to Yokohama sea lanes. During New Year's and once or twice during the summer, it also offered Yokohama to Hong Kong cruises. Our kids were excited about being on a ship for the first time, and we felt it would be enjoyable to spend New Year's in Hong Kong. It was a great experience. We greeted 1976 aboard a converted Chinese junk with other foreign expats and well-heeled Chinese folks. The New Year's celebration package that we purchased turned out to be a good deal, providing a gourmet Chinese dinner, superb entertainment, and dancing to a big band, while we the cruised the waters around Hong Kong. It, indeed, was a night to remember! The cruise itself was fun, and we quickly made friends with the Japanese and foreign passengers—who were all in high spirits. Some US servicemen from Okinawa also joined us for part of the cruise. We especially enjoyed the Russian musical entertainment on board, as well as the Russian food. (Some Americans found that food too heavy. The Japanese passengers had their own Japanese meals.) The shipboard atmosphere was quite enjoyable, and Alex and Nicky were agreeable models to the many young Japanese shutterbugs who wanted to photograph them. When Alex cut his finger onboard the ship one day, the ship's friendly Russian doctor treated his slight injury

Entertaining Japanese-style at the J&H Tokyo
employee outing in Atami.

as a major operation, and continued examining his finger
every day for about a week to make sure the wound was
healing properly. But more than Alex's finger, I think he
was interested in our family's Russian background. We
rewarded him for his excellent service to Alex by giving
him a *Playboy* magazine that someone had given us.

As expected, security was always present to ensure that
there was no unauthorized fraternization between the
Soviet crew and the foreign passengers. Apparently, the
Baikal's mission was to earn foreign currency for the state
and nothing more. Before long, however, I noticed that a
young crew member, whose name I don't recall but whom

I'll call Misha, started spending an inordinate amount of time with us and the other passengers. He even had a cabin on the same deck as the passengers. He wasn't any kind of social director, but while the rest of the stewards and crew members went about their duties, Misha spent time partying with us, the Americans and Japanese. On one particular night, Misha joined the passengers in toasting one too many vodkas and got intoxicated. We didn't see him for a couple of days, but when he returned, his demeanor was subdued. No longer was he our good time Misha! I've always wondered what his punishment was for socializing too much with us.

About two years after I arrived in Tokyo, Hal Reynolds—who had lived in Japan for many years—was transferred. Peter Skov was chosen to replace him. This turned out to be a surprise to all, as Peter's background was not in the insurance industry. Management in New York must have decided he would be a good administrator, in view of his government background and experience. I was not privy to the events leading to the management change, but shortly after Peter took over the reins of J&H Tokyo, I noticed a policy swing toward more bureaucracy in the office. For example, we received a directive outlining organizational changes, with some very imaginative titles and job descriptions. I still remember one example quite vividly, regarding the new title of our elderly, genial, mailman. He handled the pickup of incoming mail from the nearby post office, as well as collecting and stamping all outgoing office mail before he took it to the post office.

In the new administration, his title was CCO, or chief communications officer. I had to chuckle when I read that our popular mailman was now the chief communications officer! It sounded so impressive!

With Hal's departure, only two expats remained at J&H Tokyo. The accounts that Hal handled were farmed out to various account executives, and I received my share of them, including the Tokyo American Club account. I continued my regular work of servicing the various accounts that I was assigned, and was aggressively pursuing new business. By then, I was also chairing our regular production meetings, which all account executives attended. A day before the meeting, I would receive reports from all of the producers, and I would consolidate them into one report. Next day at the production meeting, everybody would provide their individual comments, based on the written reports. This management tool was very important for us, as it helped us develop short-term production tactics, as well as long-term strategic goals for the office. After all, it was "produce or perish," and production and more production was the name of the game.

From my early teenage years in Yokohama's Area I Housing Area, when I rang door bells to obtain lawn-mowing work, I learned an important lesson in life. It was, simply put, nothing ventured, nothing gained. You had to be aggressive and initiate things yourself, and in my case, it was ringing doorbells. Offering lawn-mowing services was not that much different from offering corporate-insurance services. The same principles applied. Bottom

St. Mary's annual dinner-dance. Left to right: Tania, Hiroko Grab, Willy Mahr, his wife, Grace, and I. Tokyo.

line, you had to be comfortable dealing with people and understand that the worst that could happen was that someone might say no to you. This is the thought that I always tried to impart on our young Japanese producers, especially as it was not the Japanese way of soliciting business. In the Japanese corporate environment, one normally would attempt to obtain new business via official channels. That often involved formal introductions based on long-standing business connections, interlocking corporate stock ownership, business tradeoffs, and family and other close ties. Contacting a Japanese corporate prospect out of the blue was not usually a good idea. At J&H Tokyo, it normally would not be a problem, as we were dealing with American or other foreign companies. However, the staff at these foreign firms was Japanese, and customs and traditions were hard to ignore. Still, we worked hard and had our share of successes in gaining new accounts through the cold-call method. We also obtained introductions from the J&H worldwide network to service the Japan-based portion of various worldwide insurance programs. Yet to me, the most rewarding part of being an insurance broker in Japan was developing local insurance accounts, often with no formal or corporate introduction. In short, my life as an expat insurance broker in Japan was enjoyable and active, and it provided me with a lot of opportunities to make new friends and acquaintances from all over the world. On the other hand, Tania and I often missed our family and friends in the States, as well as in Chile (where Tania's mother and other relatives lived); and we looked forward to the annual home leave, when we would be able to recharge our batteries before returning to Tokyo to resume our expat life.

As my fifth-year anniversary in Tokyo approached, I was informed that I would be transferred back to the States in June 1980. The reason given was that J&H Tokyo was scaling down its expat staff to only one, to reduce costs. It was unfortunate, as I had gotten accustomed to my work, and my future prospects looked good. Still, I didn't mind returning to San Francisco. I felt, after five years in Tokyo, it might be good for me to spend some time back in the

States. However, when I heard I was being sent to Atlanta, I knew it wouldn't work for Tania or me. In a nutshell, in the end, J&H San Francisco's international department, once again, came to my rescue. San Francisco agreed to take me back into their international department, where I would again handle some of J&H's international accounts. I would also be the Japanese resource, facilitating Japanese business development. In recent years, J&H had taken a big step in the United States vis-à-vis expanding its Japanese business portfolio, and J&H San Francisco was keen to obtain its share of it. I was pleased with this development, as I would be back among friends and I could immediately commence working on familiar accounts. I knew I would do well in San Francisco, and that it would be better to send a Japanese national to Atlanta to cultivate the growing Japanese business activity there. And eventually that's what happened.

So, in June 1980, after a heartwarming sayonara office party, hosted by the J&H Tokyo Employees Club, I received a beautifully designed farewell card, signed by all of my colleagues, together with their parting comments, and a Seiko world watch to remember them by. It was quite touching. The next day, we flew home to Calistoga, California, our summer residence in the wine country, seventy-five miles north of San Francisco. No sooner had I unpacked, I received a letter from Chubb International welcoming me back to the States. It informed me that Chubb was contemplating a change of staff in their Tokyo operation later in the year, and suggested that we stay in

Sayonara J&H Tokyo reception. I am pictured with
Mr. Ino, Claims Mgr and Miss Kuwana, June 1980.

touch. Furthermore, the company invited me to visit with
them, should I have an opportunity to be in the New York
area in the near future. The letter was a real surprise, and
I wondered what to do with it. Again, the answer to my
question came in the mail. Less than three weeks later,
I received another letter from Chubb International. This
time, its message was very clear. It confirmed that Chubb
had decided to effect a position transfer in Tokyo by the
end of the year, and that they wanted to offer me the
position of Japan representative. Was Chubb afraid that I
would accept a position from another company? So, now
I had to make another career decision, since my second
international opportunity had come knocking! To make

a long story short, I decided to accept Chubb's offer and return to Tokyo in early January 1981. Meanwhile, I would continue working at J&H San Francisco until the end of the year. Everything went smoothly and amicably, with Chubb International even coordinating my transfer back to Japan with J&H San Francisco. I was now headed back to Tokyo to assume my new position as Federal Insurance Company's Japan representative. (Federal was a member company of the Chubb group of insurance companies, and the licensed member to operate in Japan.)

CHAPTER 14
Life of an Expat in Japan, Part II

Accompanied by my family, I returned to Japan on my second tour of duty in January 1981, arriving at the new, modern Narita Tokyo International Airport aboard a United Airlines jumbo jet. As soon as we entered the crowded immigration area, we couldn't help noticing the sign that read Japanese and Aliens. All Japanese citizens lined up under the Japanese sign and all foreigners went under the aliens sign to have their passports stamped. After years of UFO jokes and negative comments, I believe the sign was eventually changed to read non-Japanese, or some other more suitable alternative. Incidentally, the internal passport that all resident foreigners in Japan must always carry is called the alien registration card. One of Webster's definitions of alien reads: "Differing in nature or character typically to the point of incompatibility." This could describe foreigners in general, as well as visitors from outer space! Were the Japanese trying to tell us, the arriving gaijins, something?

After the long limousine bus ride from the airport—Narita is approximately seventy kilometers from central Tokyo—we arrived at the swank Okura Hotel, favored by Americans and located next to the American embassy. It was to be our home for seven weeks. Why so long? Answer:

Somebody back in the States forgot about our household goods container, which was stored at an Oakland pier for weeks until, finally, after repeated follow-ups, it was located and shipped to Tokyo. But not to get ahead of the story. The day after we arrived, Tania and I met with the departing Federal Insurance Company Japan representative, the affable Jim Talley, and his charming Australian-born wife for lunch. We discussed the agenda for the next two weeks, covering our transition period, as well as various items that needed to be clarified. Before leaving for Tokyo, I had spent some time at Chubb International in New York, where Henry Parker, the director of international operations and my new boss, briefed me on the long-established Chubb-Sumitomo relationship. He also introduced me to all of Chubb International's key international players, with whom I would work in the coming weeks and months. Chubb had been managing Sumitomo Marine's US operations for a considerable time; and, in turn, Sumitomo Marine was the managing agent of Chubb's operations in Japan. Sumitomo Marine & Fire Insurance Company was a long-established company with a proud corporate history, and in Japan it ranked number four among the Japanese non-life insurance companies. It was a member of the powerful Sumitomo industrial group, which included Sumitomo Trust, Sumitomo Life Insurance, Sumitomo Bank, Sumitomo Corporation, NEC Corporation, and many other major Japanese corporate interests. As Henry Parker had instructed me earlier, my role in Tokyo could

Conferring with M&M Tokyo's Wayne Brock,
Tokyo, September 12, 1984.

be summarized as follows: (1) maintain and expand the Chubb-Sumitomo business relationship; and (2) develop Chubb's local business operation, Federal Japan, so it would become a viable, active profit center.

As Jim Talley explained during our transition discussions, his role in Japan had been as a sort of ambassador to Sumitomo Marine. Jim and his wife had charming personalities, and it was easy to work with Jim during the transition phase. He quickly introduced me to all of the Sumitomo Marine executives, as well as the key underwriting and production kachos (section chiefs), who were involved with the Federal book of business. At the time, it was mostly all coinsurance and reinsurance business referred from Sumitomo, with hardly any locally produced Federal Insurance Company business. In addition to continuing the diplomatic work with Sumitomo Marine that Jim had been involved with, my challenge was going to be in the area of direct business development and expansion. Chubb International had its share of international business all over the world, but much of the Japan-based business was handled by our competitors. My challenge was to change this state of affairs. In view of my brokerage experience at J&H Tokyo, I was uniquely qualified to work on this effort. I immediately started to set up the mechanism by which Federal Japan would become one of the active members of the family of foreign insurance companies licensed to do business in Japan. Since I was already known in the local insurance market, it was not too difficult to develop and expand our business relations with the foreign brokers and agents in Japan, as well as to maintain ties with fellow members of the Foreign Non-Life Insurance Association. (I was appointed secretary of this insurance association shortly after my arrival in Tokyo.)

Before Sumitomo Marine built its large, modern head-office building at Shinkawa 2-chome, Tokyo, in 1988, it was headquartered in Tokyo's Nihonbashi district, with a number of annexes scattered over various parts of central Tokyo. When I became Japan representative, Federal's office was located within Sumitomo Marine's overseas department, in one of the half dozen high-rises that clustered above the rest of the buildings surrounding nearby Shinjuku railway station. I think folks referred to this cluster of tall buildings as the six sisters. My gaijin neighbor within Sumitomo Marine's overseas department was the British reinsurance broker Sedgwick. I often networked with their representative, Bob Maynard, especially in connection with mutual Sumitomo-related issues. If I recall correctly, my office was on the thirty-third floor, and I remember the day the earth shook. It was a scary moment on the thirty-third floor, but fortunately, the quake didn't last long. Japan is earthquake country and prone to frequent tremors. On one occasion, I was sleeping in our Homat Amber ground-floor apartment, when another earthquake rattled the neighborhood. The jolt was so strong, it literally threw me out of bed. The third and most dramatic earthquake experience I had in Tokyo occurred while I was meeting with a client. Just before it started shaking, we were discussing the need to continue with the client's earthquake coverage. Just as the client was considering dropping the coverage due to its high cost, a strong earthquake jolted the building and lasted for about fifteen seconds. The client's face turned red, but when he recovered, he quickly agreed to renew the earthquake insurance. As they say, timing is everything!

Dealing with Sumitomo Marine vis-à-vis their referred insurance business to our company was a routine matter, and I followed my predecessor's method of regular courtesy calls on the various Sumitomo Marine business departments. For example, every Thursday afternoon I visited the Kanda underwriting department, where I would meet with the property and casualty underwriters.

Hosting Federal Japan's annual agents' Christmas party at the Tokyo American Club. From left to right, Mr. Ducheneaux, Andy Apanay, myself, Hans Thompson and Joe Gordo.

We would often drink green tea and discuss renewal coinsurance business and any other pertinent matters. The underwriters were interested in various aspects of US insurance, and we often discussed the US insurance market, the litigious climate in the United States, the products liability exposures of Japanese manufacturers in the United States, and so forth.

With the Japanese property and casualty underwriters, I usually spoke English, as they were experienced underwriters who had spent time in the United States, Singapore, or other English-speaking countries. They enjoyed practicing their English with me. At other times, when I visited Sumitomo's Nihonbashi production department, which handled Federal's direct business, I usually spoke Japanese. Their underwriters were not proficient in English and preferred to speak in Japanese. In fact, I remember how one young production department member characterized my Japanese conversational skills. "Lavrov-san speaks Japanese, except when he gets angry. Then he switches to English!" Very observant, I thought.

In retrospect, I must say that my dealings with the Sumitomo Marine staff members generally went smoothly, especially as our representative office got organized and the Sumitomo Marine underwriters became accustomed to our foreign clients' needs. This didn't happen overnight. First, I required a Japanese assistant (my right hand, as they say), whose responsibility was to deal with the daily nuts and bolts of handling the placements of Federal's direct business. During my time at Federal Japan, I had two Japanese right hand male assistants working for me. Unfortunately, with the first English-speaking assistant, who was trained in the United States but had no experience in the local Japanese insurance market, things did not work out. The second assistant, who was local, had extensive casualty insurance experience working for a Tokyo-based foreign underwriter. His English was weak, but he was able to provide me with good support; and, as our volume of direct business grew, his assistance became crucial. He maintained close daily contact, not only with the Sumitomo production and underwriting team that serviced Federal's business, but also worked well with the Japanese staff of the foreign brokers and agents.

One business practice in Japanese firms, including Sumitomo Marine, that didn't make our work any easier, was the tradition of transferring employees from one department to another each April first, when the new fiscal year began. For example, our Sumitomo underwriter liaison might be transferred to an overseas post, and a newcomer from the production department would replace him. I understood the purpose behind it was to broaden the employees' experience, but to us it meant we had to spend more time in developing rapport with the new representatives, as well as introducing them to our foreign book of business. This added work took time away from our regular workload. As small as Federal Japan was, we had little time to spare. Still, we pressed on, and eventually, I moved our office from the shared Sumitomo premises in Nihonbashi to a new and larger Federal Insurance Company representative office next to the Akasaka district, and close to where the Japanese Diet (Parliament) is located. Our staff consisted of me (the foreign representative), my Japanese assistant, plus an office secretary. In addition, we had a young Sumitomo Marine production representative who daily spent about four hours in our office. He was Sumitomo's official working-level liaison representative to Federal, who reviewed and processed Federal applications with our Japanese manager. Federal's local business was growing, the future looked promising, and we were contemplating upgrading Federal's representative office status to that of a full branch operation in the near future.

Public relations were an important part of my job, and I was busy promoting Federal in every way I could. For example, I would frequently prepare and forward company press releases to the English language newspapers. The announcements would report Chubb senior executives' Tokyo visits, the introduction of new Federal insurance products into the Japanese insurance market, as well as other information that might interest the foreign business community. I also arranged cocktail receptions at various venues for both Chubb and Sumitomo Marine executive and senior staff. These were rather formal occasions, with local protocol strictly followed. As is popular in Japan, we hosted annual Christmas parties for our producers at the Tokyo American Club. And I was a frequent guest at numerous corporate and embassy receptions, where I could fly the Federal flag. All of this activity kept Federal in the limelight and created a positive image for our company.

On weekends, Tania and I did our shopping at National Azabu, Kinokuniya, and other Tokyo supermarkets frequented by gaijins, and on Sundays our family would attend Nikolai-do services. One bright Sunday morning in the fall of 1982, I happened to go alone to church, where I had the great honor of meeting, unexpectedly, one of Russia's greatest writers, the legendary Alexander Solzhenitsyn. He had traveled to Japan from America, incognito, to make a presentation to a Japanese organization in Tokyo and to tour the country. On this particular day, he chose to visit Nikolai-do Cathedral for the Sunday service. Before he entered the cathedral, he spent some time in the church courtyard, where I spotted him standing alone, dressed in simple cotton garb. A lean middle-aged Japanese bodyguard, in suit and tie, and with an electronic earpiece, hovered around him. I couldn't resist meeting Solzhenitsyn, and as I approached him, I noticed the tense bodyguard moving closer and closer to him. As I came right up to the famous author of the *Gulag Archipelago, August 1914, The First Circle*, and other great works, the guard's body language flashed *attack mode*. He was ready to karate chop me in a split second should I make any hostile moves against the writer. Speaking Russian, I introduced myself, telling him who I was and what I was doing in Japan. Shaking his hand warmly, I told him how much I admired him, not only for his writing but for courageously standing up to the authoritarian Soviets. He responded very kindly, asked a few questions, and shortly thereafter entered the cathedral. Not long after, I also went inside the church and saw him praying on his knees in front of the altar. When Tania heard that I had met Alexander Solzhenitsyn at church that day, she was very disappointed that she hadn't been with me. My only regret was that I didn't have my camera. But Tania got her opportunity to meet another VIP after Easter midnight services at Nikolai-do on Sunday, April 22, 1984. In fact, it was Alexander Solzhenitsyn's friend and fellow Russian dissident, Mstislav Rostropovich, the world-famous cellist and orchestra maestro. He was visiting Tokyo on a concert tour, and had come to the midnight Easter service at the cathedral, where some of us gaijins met him. After the service, and as was the custom, we invited him and a group of friends to our Homat Amber apartment in Ichibancho. We clicked colored Easter eggs to see which ones would break (a Russian tradition); ate Easter bread, called kulich; and toasted Easter with shots of Stolichnaya vodka. This time, Tania got her picture with Slava, the famous maestro!

Most of my work at Federal Japan centered in Tokyo, but occasionally I would take the train to Yokohama, where my friend and fellow St. Joseph alumnus, Joe Gordo, managed Rollins, Heath's (RH) local office. RH was one of the large foreign insurance brokers in Japan with which Federal had an agency agreement. Joe was very active in local insurance circles, and I kept in close touch with him and with his Tokyo-based boss and fellow SJC alumnus, Andy Apanay. Occasionally, I would travel by bullet train to the Kobe/Osaka area, mainly to visit Sumitomo Marine, Osaka; but also to call on some of our Kansai clients, agents, and prospects. Once, when I visited Osaka, I made a presentation to the American Chamber of Commerce in Japan's (ACCJ's) local branch, where I spoke on personal insurance for the foreign expat. In Tokyo, I was on ACCJ's employment practices committee, as well as on the China committee. From time to time, I wrote articles for the chamber's monthly journal. At the Tokyo American Club (TAC), I was a member of the house committee (1976–1978), as well as on the safety committee (1979–1980), where I served as chairman in 1979. I also ran, unsuccessfully, for a seat on TAC's Board of Governors for the 1983–1985 term.

After about five years at Federal Japan, and as we were working on upgrading our representative office operations to independent branch status, a major change occurred at Chubb International's headquarters in Warren, New Jersey. A new man replaced my boss as director of Chubb's international operations, and Henry Parker, "Mr. International," who was the most knowledgeable and experienced international executive at Chubb, assumed new non-international responsibilities. This development was sudden and unexpected, and in faraway Tokyo, I was not privy to the details. Shortly after, I started noticing trends that indicated a shift toward more corporate bureaucracy, with Chubb Singapore, the regional center of Chubb's Asian network, taking a more active stance vis-à-vis Federal Japan. In previous years, Federal Japan's operations were managed on a more direct basis; i.e., Federal Tokyo–Chubb Warren, NJ, head office. Now, it increasingly became Tokyo–Singapore–Warren. This additional layer of bureaucracy only complicated matters and, in my view, was counterproductive. I felt that, perhaps after Federal Japan received its branch license and was operating as a 100 percent Chubb owned and operated entity, then would be a better time to have Federal Tokyo report to Singapore. But it was not for me to decide.

In any event, with the major executive personnel shifts at Chubb International, the winds of change were blowing our way, and I could sense that the time had come for me to consider returning to the States. After I bit the bullet and requested a transfer, I didn't hear from head office for

Russian Easter celebration. From left to right, myself,
Mstislav Rostropovich, the world renowned cellist and conductor,
Tania and Natalie Ermakoff, Tokyo, April, 22, 1984.

a long time. Was I being sent to Coventry? I wondered.
Finally, after a considerable period of time, I received the
official announcement that I was being rotated to the
overseas investors department in the Warren, New Jersey,
head office. There, I would join a number of underwriters
servicing Japanese businesses that Chubb was managing
for Sumitomo Marine in the United States. When my
colleagues at Sumitomo Marine heard this news, they
were supportive, but they understood that it wasn't a
promotion for me. In fact, one senior Sumitomo executive
discreetly pulled me aside at a reception one evening and
remarked that Chubb was losing my talent in Japan. He
knew me well and was aware of my successful business

contributions to Federal's growth in Japan. Soon after, in May 1986, my replacement, David French, a new hire at Chubb International, arrived on the scene, and, as they say, the rest is history.

CHAPTER 15
Doing Business in Japan

"East is East, and West is West." We've all heard this cliché about the differences between the Oriental and the Occidental world. While it's true there are differences, the Western businessman can learn to adapt to and prosper in dealing with his Japanese counterparts, be it in the Land of the Rising Sun, the United States, or anywhere in the world. My personal expat experience of more than ten years of working in Japan attests to that. Following is a list of dos and don'ts of doing business with the Japanese that I drafted a long time ago, but it is still relevant today. It includes simple, common-sense suggestions that could apply anywhere in the world, but it's amazing how many foreign businessmen have never heard of them, much less followed them. The first section that follows stresses the positive elements that one should consider; the second part outlines the negative factors that should be avoided.

What to do when dealing with the Japanese:

1. Always be punctual. A 10 a.m. business appointment with a Japanese client means exactly 10 a.m. Not 9:45 or 10:30. Japan is not a South American country where it's fashionable to arrive late. Make sure you have a dependable watch set for the correct time.

2. Always be well prepared. The Japanese always do their homework and expect you to do the same. They will quickly notice, for example, if you do not know your numbers. Arrive at the meeting with a stack of notes, slides, or pamphlets that will enable you to negotiate professionally and to the point. Ask lots of pertinent questions.

3. Always be patient. Understand that decision making in corporate Japan requires nemawashi (consensus), and involves a time-consuming process. Japanese management decisions are not made from top to bottom, as we are familiar with back home. For example, when you make an offer to a Japanese businessman, he will pass it on to a group of his senior colleagues to review and sign off on. This process is often lengthy and time consuming. Only when all are in agreement, can he reply to you with his firm's response.

4. Always start with small talk. The standard courtesy extended to guests in Japan is for the receptionist to bring you inside the reception or conference room. She will ask you if you prefer tea (often green tea) or coffee. She will then disappear and quickly return with the refreshments. By then, the Japanese businessmen you came to meet will have arrived; and before sitting down, they will exchange their meishi (business cards) with you. The local executives will bow slightly and solemnly present their cards to you. (These cards are often printed in Japanese and English.) You, as the foreign guest, should reciprocate in a similar manner, preferably with bilingual business cards of your own. A brief period of small talk generally precedes the main discussion. For example, the Japanese side might ask you where you are staying while in Tokyo, the duration of your visit, how a colleague whom they met previously is doing, and so forth. The small talk is designed to create a friendly atmosphere prior to the important business discussion.

5. Listen. It's important for the American or foreign guest not only to present his business pitch, but to politely listen to his Japanese hosts' comments or questions. Listening indicates that you are alert and interested in your hosts' ideas and concerns. It's also important for you to raise questions and comments, so that a smooth pattern of enquiry can be followed. But make sure to never monopolize the discussion. Doing so will guarantee a negative reaction from the Japanese side. In any event, if your first meeting goes well, you will have many more opportunities regarding your proposal.

6. Always act courteously. Courtesy plays an important role in traditional Japanese society, and no less in the local business environment. For starters, it's important to learn at least a few Japanese words, like domo arigato (thank you), hajime mashita (pleased to meet you), and what the Japanese say at the end of meetings: yoroshiku onegai tashimasu, which literally means, let's work amicably together. A slight bow, together with a handshake, is also appropriate when saying hello or good-bye. While most Japanese businesspeople know at least some English (English is a mandatory subject at Japanese high schools), your use of some Japanese words and phrases will impress them and make a difference. The more courteous you are in Japan, the more opportunities you will have opened to you. But what about when *yes* in Japan may still mean *no*. The short answer is to put whatever was agreed to in writing. It's always important to document any agreements reached, even tentative ones. Many Japanese businessmen can write English better than they can speak it. Once they receive your confirmation letter, you can be sure that they will understand it.

7. Persistence pays. The Japanese may appear to be quiet, courteous folks, but when it comes to business negotiations, they can be fearless tigers. (Hence, their nickname of corporate warriors.) After all, it's in their nature to ganbatte, meaning, to keep fighting and never give up. And if you're a worthy competitor, they expect you to be as dogged as they are. So, in dealing with the Japanese, always keep following up and never quickly give in. Sooner or later, you will be successful, and both sides can enjoy a mutually beneficial relationship.

8. Thank-you letters are a must. This practice is one of the easiest to follow, yet it's amazing how many folks ignore it or don't think about it. From my own experience, I can state unequivocally how important thank-you letters have been in my work. I would write these letters after every visit to a client or prospect. They were simple letters, confirming the meeting we had, the subject we covered, the hope for a mutual business opportunity in the future, any tentative agreements discussed, and the like. Just as I would think my Japanese client had forgotten me, I would receive his letter in response, providing me with another window of opportunity.

9. Always use surnames. One reason why business cards are so important with the Japanese is that they provide you with valuable information that you need to deal effectively with them. On a typical Japanese business card, not only will you find the first and last names of the individual, you'll also have his or her title—an important detail to include, especially on letters and documents. (The Japanese side of the business card will also have the specific Japanese characters for the individual's name.) Always orally address your Japanese associates or clients by their surnames, regardless of gender, and add *san* (a term of respect) after their last name. (E.g., Yamashita-san.) Never call them by their first names. Generally, if you are writing in English, include their full name; e.g., Mr. Ichiro Yamashita, Miss Junko Kagawa, or Mrs. Atsuko Sato. During the '70s and '80s, Ms. was not commonly used in Japan. Mixing up names and titles is a big no-no in Japan, and foreigners and Japanese alike pay close attention to this detail, meticulously keeping track of corporate personnel changes.

10. Always carry sufficient business cards, which are the Japanese businessman's corporate identification. How many times have I met with American clients in the States and they've forgotten to bring their business cards? I would estimate at least 50 percent of the time. This rarely happens with the Japanese. Over the years,

Taking a break between sales calls in Yokohama.

I've had my share of overseas associates come to Japan minus their business cards. Not only was it embarrassing in front of senior Japanese management personnel, it was also counterproductive. Business cards had to be mailed later, with our apologies. This did not create a favorable impression on our Japanese hosts. Just like you check your wallet and watch when you dress in the morning, remember to make sure you always have a sufficient supply of business cards. (Plus an additional supply in your attaché case, just in case.)

11. Always pay the bill. How many times have we heard foreign businessmen on their first visit to Japan sing their praises of the Japanese? "They were so gracious and always paid the bill!" Yes, they paid the bill because they were polite, but it's you, dummy, who should have paid the bill if you were eager to do business with them. After all, when we want to impress someone back home, aren't we the ones who invite the prospective clients for lunch or dinner, with the tacit understanding that we are doing the treating? I've heard locals complain about the ugly foreign businessmen who had large appetites but apparently small wallets, as the Japanese ended up paying for them. Japan is an expensive place, especially for any high-class entertaining. If you want to do business in Japan, make sure you have a lot of yen for your entertainment expenses, and leave the dollars at home. Always plan where you will be entertaining, what your expense account budget should be, and remember to always pay the bill, even if your Japanese guests attempt to take the bill away from you.

What not to do when dealing with the Japanese:

1. Don't try to be funny. You've probably heard about the Midwesterner on his first business trip to Japan. He arranged to have an early 9 a.m. meeting with a large group of Japanese businessmen. He liked to crack jokes back home, and thought a little humor would be the best way to introduce him and his company to the sleepy salarymen. After he laughingly related his tale, he waited for a moment to hear the response. But there was no reaction whatsoever. The entire group remained stone-faced and silent. What had gone wrong? he thought. Apparently, no one had warned the gentleman that when it comes to intercultural exchanges, being funny and telling jokes generally doesn't work in Japan. While most Japanese know some English, their comprehension of the language usually does not extend to understanding American humor. In this situation, "East is East, and West is West" indeed, and we are not on the same wave-length. Save the jokes for the folks back home.

2. Avoid slang. This is similar to rule number one above. The only English that should be used with the Japanese is international English—English words that are most common and universally understood and accepted. Speak slowly and try to pronounce each word as clearly as possible. Remember, the Japanese businessman's English is not on par with yours, and he needs time to translate every word into Japanese. His brain must then process the information in Japanese. The final step is for him to translate his Japanese response into English, so you can understand him.

3. Don't promote yourself to your clients. The Japanese work in a group-oriented environment, and everything revolves around their company. The typical Japanese salaryman spends almost all of his time on weekdays working at the company; and on weekends, he often spends additional time involved in extracurricular activities related to the firm. His only free time usually is on Sunday, when he can catch up on his sleep before spending time with his family. You'll notice the Japanese frequently use the word we instead of I. They proudly wear their company pin on their suit lapels, and introduce themselves as "I am company XYZ's Yamada." It's almost never, "I am Yamada, pleased to meet you." For them, the company always comes first!

4. Don't appear out of the blue! It is not an accepted practice to arrive at a Japanese business without making prior arrangements to see someone. Not only is it considered rude, it is also very unprofessional. Plus, the Japanese like to do their homework before they decide to meet with anybody. Even if you've already been introduced to them, you must follow the proper business etiquette of setting up an appointment. For example, if you are visiting Japan and are contacting a new prospect, make sure your letter clearly states the purpose of your visit, the name(s) of the representatives who will attend, and other pertinent details. Ideally, the latest annual report, or at least a fact sheet on your firm's current operations, should be enclosed. Otherwise, be prepared to receive a rejection, or even worse, no reply at all.

5. Dress appropriately. While the Japanese businessmen do not wear uniforms, they all dress more or less alike, in a conservative suit with dress shirt and tie. A Japanese saying which is apropos in this instance states: "The nail that stands out must be hammered in." I recall one occasion when a senior American businessman visited Japan and forgot to bring his business suit. He visited a number of high-ranking Japanese executives, who were shocked to meet him, dressed as if he had come to a Hawaiian luau. This foreign visitor was the talk of the town on the local business grapevine.

6. Never promise anything you can't deliver. Japanese executives diligently prepare for their overseas visitors, and they expect their visitors to do the same. Don't expect your junior managers to be able to meet with high-ranking executives, as the Japanese follow protocol meticulously. In fact, it might take several meetings at the lower level before a meeting with top executives can be achieved. And then, it's important that the foreigners come prepared and with the authority to negotiate and make agreements. The worst case scenario is when juniors (or even seniors) promise to perform a contract, but then renege on it. This creates loss of face and lost opportunities.

7. Avoid doing business from a distance. Develop a personal relationship with your client. While much business is done by phone and correspondence, it's important the gaijin businessman regularly meets with his Japanese counterpart on a face-to-face basis. If he is from overseas, he should plan a visit to Japan at least once a year, and perhaps even more. If he is a Tokyo-based expat, he should regularly call on his Japanese client. Getting to know your client solidifies the relationship and opens the door for future business opportunities.

8. Know your client's title. One of the worst faux pas that you can make dealing with the Japanese is to mix up somebody's title. The Japanese take their corporate titles seriously, so use great care when official correspondence is prepared, to ensure the correct name and title is used.

9. Avoid staring into someone's eyes. In America and other parts of the world, eye contact with your clients, or people in general, is highly encouraged. In Japan, it's considered rude to stare into another's eyes. Accordingly, care must be exercised during meetings so as not to give the impression that you are gazing into anyone's eyes. This doesn't mean you must totally avoid eye contact. Just avoid looking directly into someone's eyes for too long. Move your eyes around.

10. Avoid giving gifts that are not properly wrapped. Gift giving is very popular in Japan, and is almost an art in itself. Twice a year, including at New Years, gifts are exchanged among the locals. When foreign visitors come to Japan to visit their business associates, it is customary to exchange gifts. The Japanese make a big effort in choosing the right gift, as well as making sure that the wrapping is immaculate. Americans don't attach much significance to wrapping paper or how a gift is wrapped. But they should, because if the gift is poorly wrapped, it creates a poor impression of you with the Japanese. They'll probably forget the gift, but they will always remember how poorly it was wrapped.

I developed the above dos and don'ts primarily for my American colleagues, to help them avoid the label "Ugly American" and to assist them in developing Japanese business in Japan, as well as in the United States. Working in Japan and elsewhere in the world requires adjusting, not only to the local business climate, but much more. Every place is different and, as expats, we have many challenges, not the least of which is to be on top of the historical and cultural traditions and mores of the local people. While some of the above rules of doing business in Japan might appear insignificant, in my Japanese business experience, knowing and practicing them really works.

CHAPTER 16
Back in the USA

At the completion of my second Japanese expat assignment in June 1986, I flew Japan Airlines straight to San Francisco and our summer cottage in Calistoga. A few days later, Tania and the kids left Japan for Hawaii and a short vacation in Waikiki. While soaking up the sun in the wine country, I spent time catching up on family matters with my parents, and pondered what my new life would be at Chubb in Warren, New Jersey. Our household goods were shipped directly to the New York area, so until we settled into our new residence on the East Coast, my family and I would be living out of our suitcases. By early July, my vacation was over. I flew to Newark, New Jersey, and checked into my hotel, some miles from the Chubb office. Meanwhile, my family would continue to enjoy summer in Calistoga and the Russian River area until early September. Then, Tania and Nick would join me in New Jersey. Alex had been accepted as an electrical engineering student at Loyola Marymount University in Los Angeles, and he would live there on campus. My stay at the local hotel would last a few weeks, after which I would move to one of Chubb's well-maintained corporate condos, located a few miles from the office. Soon after my arrival in New Jersey, I purchased a new Nova four-door sedan. I now had wheels, and didn't feel so isolated due to the lack of public transportation in the area. New Jersey is called the Garden State for its beautiful parks and greenery, which you notice as you drive along its turnpike and highways. Another thing I observed was the numerous tollbooths in the area. It seemed you had to pay for every few miles you drove. Coming from California, with its extensive network of toll-free freeways, it was a surprise for me.

With its well-designed modern buildings and beautifully landscaped grounds, Chubb's home office complex in Warren resembled a college campus. As the campus was in somewhat of an isolated area, without any hotels, shopping centers, or convenient public transportation, it was designed to be a self-contained facility where employees could spend their whole day at the office. Not only was there plenty of modern office space, but its center area was designed as a hub, complete with a bank, gift store, dry cleaning shop, and library. There was also a large cafeteria, which was well patronized during the day. During the summer, Chubb's employees would often have their lunches on the well-maintained lawns.

It was at this idyllic setting that I arrived one July morning. As a first step, I paid my respects to Bob Lynyak, director and general manager of the International Department. After that, I spent time discussing some of my personal matters, including the house search I was going to undertake. Chubb's relocation specialist provided me with the necessary introduction to a local rental agency, whose representative promised to assist me with my search. After that, I was introduced to my new colleagues in the overseas investors department (OID), who worked on insurance programs for Japanese-owned corporations that were located in the United States, mainly involving the Sumitomo group of companies. The manager of this unit was a tall, slim gentleman in his thirties, whose name, unfortunately, I do not recall. In any event, he briefed me on the operations of the OID and introduced me to his assistant, as well as to the other members of the "reverse-flow" business team. I was handed a list of the Japanese accounts that I would be responsible for, and shortly after, I set to work. This was an underwriting position, and I would work on insurance programs being renewed or, in some way, requiring service. It would be my responsibility to make sure that Chubb's underwriting requirements were being adhered to. Similarly, in the case of new Japanese business, applications had to be checked and rated, and policies issued. Compared to the exciting hustle and bustle of new business development that I had been used to back in Japan, or even in San Francisco, working on the underwriting side in Warren was rather mundane. Still, I accepted it as a new challenge to be added to my overall reservoir of insurance knowledge.

By early August, I had leased a split-level three-bedroom house in New Providence, New Jersey, which was located about thirty minutes from the office. By mid-August, our household goods container had arrived, and I hurriedly unpacked our belongings. I wanted to have the house more or less ready for my family when they arrived at the end of August. Fortunately, New Providence High School, recommended by friends, was nearby, and upon arrival, Nick was enrolled there as a freshman. Sometime later, in order to update my knowledge of US insurance practices, Chubb International's management enrolled me in a two-month property/casualty insurance study program at the "insurance college" at the head office. This was a full-time classroom program covering the main lines of US property-casualty insurance. It was like going back to college to bone up on American insurance practices. I enjoyed the courses and passed the final exam without much difficulty. Meanwhile, Tania, and to some degree, Nick, were experiencing reverse culture shock. Although I'd often traveled to New York on business trips, we had never lived on the East Coast, and Tania was finding life in New Jersey in general, and New Providence in particular, dull and depressing. She missed her friends in Tokyo and San Francisco. Fortunately, she soon found a part-time job that kept her busy. Slowly but surely, she began adjusting to life in the Garden State. Eventually, she made new friends and life in New Jersey became more interesting.

Our family's East Coast Odyssey, as I named it, had commenced, and we started to take trips in and around New Jersey. Our plan was to see as much of New Jersey and the East Coast as our time would allow. On Saturdays, we would drive to some of the nearby towns, including Summit, where we would do our shopping. On Sundays, we would travel to Nyack, New York, home of the local Russian-American community. There, we would attend morning church services, and in the afternoon, Nick would receive his Russian lesson from an elderly Russian lady tutor. In the fall, we drove to Washington, DC, to visit the White House, the Capitol, Arlington Cemetery, and many other historic and scenic places. On the way to Washington, we stopped by Philadelphia to see historic sites there. During the Thanksgiving holidays, Alex visited us from college, and he, Nick and I drove to the Pocono Mountains, where the boys enjoyed skiing.

As our East Coast Odyssey continued, we discussed the idea of moving back to the San Francisco area the following summer. While I could handle the new underwriting job, it didn't provide me with the challenges that I sought. Working at the campus was fine, but I viewed it more as a transitional phase in my overall business career. As for my family, one year in New Jersey would be more than enough. They longed to return home to California. And so, as I was looking over the *Wall Street Journal's* classified ads section one day in October 1986, I came across a large, interesting help wanted advertisement placed by an insurance brokerage firm called Corroon & Black (C&B), a firm I had never heard of before. They were looking for an immediate Pacific Rim business development account executive to be based in their San Francisco office. Although they were not known to me, two key elements in the ad spiked my attention: Pacific Rim and San Francisco. I felt, instinctively, that this position was for me. I quickly prepared my resumé and mailed it to C&B San Francisco. Could this be my third international business opportunity and my ticket back to San Francisco?

Within a short time, I received a letter from Corroon & Black International (CBI), inviting me to meet with their international executives in New York to discuss my job application. A couple of days later, I took a day off from work and traveled to CBI New York's office in the Wall Street area. There, I was introduced to the president of CBI, Marnix Guillaume, a dapper Belgian-American, originally from the French-speaking part of Belgium, and his "right hand," the executive vice president of international, Howard Hupp, a native of the New York/ New Jersey area. Both gentlemen were very cordial, and I immediately took a liking to both of them. I learned from them that CBI was expanding worldwide, and that one particular business segment they wanted to see grow was their Japanese business share in the United States. CBI was trying to catch up to the other major brokers, like Marsh & McLennan and Johnson & Higgins, and was looking for an experienced Japanese business-development specialist to spearhead the project. They wanted a Japanese-speaking insurance resource who would develop a reverse-flow marketing plan for the United States, as well as organize and support a team of Corroon & Black account executives, with whom he would work closely. Upon learning of my family background and insurance experience, they were impressed. Our introductory meeting lasted a significant amount of time, and I thought it went very well. Prior to the next meeting, they asked me to provide CBI with a plan, together with my recommendations.

Within a week or two, I met again with Messrs. Guillaume and Hupp and provided them with my comprehensive report. Soon after, I was offered the San Francisco position, to be effective in January 1987. I accepted their offer with pleasure, and thanked them for their confidence and trust in me. I felt enthused and excited about this new job, and couldn't wait to get home to tell the good news to my family. It was agreed at the meeting that, prior to starting work at Corroon & Black San Francisco, I would spend a couple of weeks at the New York home office. This short orientation period would allow me the opportunity to meet Corroon & Black senior management and international team members, as well as obtain the necessary introduction to C&B's local and international operations. When I got home and told Tania and Nick the good news, that we would be moving back to San Francisco, they were ecstatic. I explained to them that I would leave first on a six-month temporary duty in San Francisco, during which the company would provide me with a small apartment while I organized the new international unit. Tania and Nick would join me in July. This would allow Nick to complete ninth grade at New Providence High, and give us plenty of time to plan and arrange our moving details. Meanwhile, I would stop over at home in New Providence every time I traveled to the East Coast on business. While our family would be split up for about six months, the end result would have us all back together in San Francisco in early July 1987.

The next day, I tendered my resignation letter to the head of Chubb's International Department, Bob Lynyak, and we agreed on the day of my departure from Chubb. I thanked him for everything Chubb had done for me, and told him that I looked forward to collaborating with Chubb in the future regarding US-based Japanese business, including Sumitomo businesses. Almost immediately, word spread within the international department that I was leaving the company, and it seemed that everybody was eager to wish me good luck and all the best. My final stop before I left Chubb was to the executive floor, where Henry Parker's office was located and where I conveyed my heartfelt sayonara to him. While neither of us said much during that farewell meeting, the body language said it all. It was rather a sad day for me, as Henry had hired me for the Tokyo post and we had worked very effectively during the earlier five years. Henry was a gentleman and scholar, and a real inspiration to me. It's no exaggeration to say that it was a joy working with him. He understood why I was leaving Chubb, and wished me success at CBI.

My six months at Chubb Warren provided me with a good glimpse of the East Coast, especially the New York/New Jersey area. Looking back, I have to say it worked out well for me. I got to know how folks lived and worked on the eastern seaboard, and this helped me better understand them. There were a few things that I wasn't crazy about on the East Coast. Winters are cold, and clearing the snow from the driveway every other morning wasn't much fun. I also didn't care for the high humidity in the summer. For my wife and son, who spent ten months in New Jersey, living there was thrust upon them, and they did their best until they were back home in San Francisco. For better or worse, our sojourn in New Jersey was part of the overall expat's family experience. While we weren't exactly gaijins in New Jersey, it was a new and different environment for us. On July 1, 1987, Tania and Nick returned to the West Coast and, together with Alex, who was on summer vacation from college, we settled down in Marin County, close to San Francisco. Our East Coast Odyssey had come to an end.

Celebrating our 25th Wedding Anniversary at the
Holy Virgin Community Hall, San Francisco, June 1992.

CHAPTER 17
Japanese Resource

I returned permanently to foggy San Francisco in early January 1987 to establish Corroon & Black International's Asian/Pacific unit, and became its sole corporate Japanese resource. Although I was going to concentrate on Japanese business development, the hope was that we would also be able to acquire other US-based Asian business. The plan, as envisioned by CBI New York, was to eventually hire a second individual in the new San Francisco-based international unit. This new hire would assist the various West Coast offices with the acquisition of multinational accounts involving US firms with operations abroad. My initial responsibility was to work with all Corroon & Black representatives nationwide, to introduce their representatives to Japanese and other Asian firms, and to help them obtain a fair share of this business. Under any circumstances, this was a tall order for a single individual to undertake, as Corroon & Black was the sixth largest US insurance broker, and had one or more offices in every state of the union. Japanese corporations had started building their US manufacturing plants about ten years earlier, and our major competitors had already obtained a significant percentage of the insurance for these large companies. CBI had entered the Japanese market late.

One of my first priorities was to develop a nationwide marketing strategy to pinpoint areas of Japanese business concentration, as well as to identify key Corroon & Black offices that would be working with me. In support of this production campaign, and since we were starting from scratch, we urgently required the tools necessary to deal with Japanese prospects on a day-to-day basis. As a first step, I hired a Japanese woman who would assist me by translating Japanese trade journal information, as well as performing various administrative functions. Also, as I would be traveling a significant part of my time, I needed her to be my link at the office. (This was before the era of cell phones.) Ms. Matsumoto, a short, bubbly young woman with boundless energy, was a delight to work with. She was bilingual, and did a marvelous job providing me with English translations of Japanese news clippings regarding incoming Japanese investments, along with additional research material. I was able to analyze this information and, together with my input, inform the various C&B offices of the market intelligence. Over time, my office developed an extensive data bank of new Japanese business opportunities, which we constantly updated.

Our local offices appreciated this marketing intelligence and, in turn, provided me with information obtained from their end. Before long, this constant flow of business leads provided us with numerous new business opportunities. It kept me busy, accompanying our local brokerage service personnel on calls to various new and existing Japanese

With my secretary, Ms. Matsumoto (center) and her friend
from Japan, San Francisco, December 11, 1990.

firms on the West Coast and elsewhere in the United
States. Initially, we spent a lot of time developing the tools
necessary to work with Japanese clients. For example, with
all the prospect calls we were making, we urgently required
an introductory brochure in Japanese that would present
Corroon & Black International to the Japanese market. It
needed to be a well-designed brochure, with color photos
and illustrations highlighting our corporate organization,
international network, Tokyo office, and other important
details. This urgent marketing tool was quickly designed
and printed, and, from day one, became our principal
sales tool. Without it, it would have been very difficult to
do business with Japanese prospects, especially those with
whom we were meeting for the first time. CBI also required

a Tokyo retail servicing facility for our US corporate clients with Japanese facilities, and I worked on this project as well. Through my earlier Tokyo business connections, I was able to arrange a correspondent relationship for CBI with a large Japanese insurance agency that was part of a major, well-respected bank group. This relationship was a success and lasted a number of years, until we opened our own independent Tokyo office.

What kind of work did the Japanese resource perform and what were his responsibilities? Was he a Japanese resource, a Japanese business facilitator, or a Japanese business consultant? The answer to the above questions is that he was all of those things. It was not always easy to define, succinctly, what the resource did, and management had a hard time in dealing with that when drawing up goals and objectives for the annual performance reviews. What the Japanese resource did *not* do was produce Japanese business. Occasionally, sort of by default, he might obtain an account on a personal introduction, but it was quickly assigned to one of the account executives, who would service the business. The reason for this was due to the contractual relationship that existed between the resource (the employee) and CBI (the employer.) Although he was licensed by the state insurance department to sell insurance products, the resource was not an insurance salesman. Instead, he helped the local Corroon & Black brokerage personnel to obtain the business. He did not own the business, nor did he service it. The function of the resource was to assist the account executive to make contact with Japanese firms and work together to obtain their insurance programs. Upon acquisition of the business, he would also make sure that the account was properly serviced. It's important to mention that with Japanese business development, winning major corporate accounts often took years. We, therefore, had to be prepared to think from a long-term standpoint.

Occasionally, the Japanese resource would be a troubleshooter, called to fix problems involving Japanese accounts. This was not a frequent occurrence, but when difficulties arose, the Japanese resource's assistance could be crucial. He would also perform as an inter-cultural sensei (a sort of Japanese guru), providing the local account executives with insight into proper Japanese business etiquette, customs, and traditions. For example, I often recited my "Dos and Don'ts of Doing Business with the Japanese" to prepare the local account executives for dealing with Japanese businessmen. Occasionally, I would write articles on insurance requirements for Japanese firms in the United States and, generally, promote CBI's Japanese and international network capabilities. In addition, I would speak at public forums on subjects affecting the insurance industry.

As I've already stated, titles are important to the Japanese, and at the start of my CBI career, my title was assistant vice president. Later, as management followed my progress in working with the Pacific Division's construction account executives, as well as with the numerous non-construction personnel, not only in San Francisco, but in Los Angeles,

Seattle, Portland, Anchorage, and other places, I was promoted to vice president. I developed excellent rapport with the men and women I worked with, and it is mostly due to them that my unit was successful in obtaining major Japanese construction, as well as manufacturing, pharmaceutical, airline, marine-related industries, and various other accounts.

I realized early in my time with CBI that I had two customers to serve. The first, and most obvious, was the Japanese prospect. The second and just as important was the local Corroon & Black office, which provided me with the team to handle the day-to-day servicing that a new account required. My track record on the West Coast during the first three years was appreciated by management, and I was promoted to senior vice president. I also received The Robert F. Corroon Award, signed by Robert F. Corroon, chairman of the board, and J. Bransford Wallace, chairman, brokerage services group. It read as follows:

The Robert F. Corroon Award is presented to George Lavrov, C&B San Francisco, for dedication and commitment to providing the highest quality professional service and for outstanding production excellence in 1989.

This most welcome recognition of my achievements gave me a big morale boost. I was pleased and looked forward to working for CBI for many years. While the work was fast paced, even hectic at times, and required a lot of travel within the continental United States, as well as occasionally to Alaska, Hawaii, Tokyo, and beyond, I had become accustomed to it. I think the main reason why I liked the job was the opportunity it provided to work with people from various parts of the United States and overseas. I have always been a people person, and I enjoyed meeting and developing friendly business relations, especially in international settings.

After my initial work on CBI's big picture, as it were, including its nationwide Japanese business strategy and Japanese business network, I gradually settled into my role as the Western States Japanese business resource, headquartered in San Francisco. My territory now covered about a third of the lower forty-eight states, plus Hawaii and Alaska—a much more manageable territory than with what I was originally tasked. I labored hard to obtain Japanese accounts for our western offices and, at the same time, concentrated on cementing close relations with the various CBI office managers and staff. This two-pronged strategy proved effective, with our Western offices obtaining significant Japanese business over the years. And good business results equated significant annual production bonuses.

As Corroon & Black's US and overseas operations grew, mainly by acquiring smaller insurance brokerage firms, it took on one of the usual characteristics of a large corporation. It became more and more bureaucratic. One day in the early 1990s, with a merger and acquisition frenzy in the insurance industry in full swing, Corroon & Black was acquired by Willis Faber, one of the world's largest insurance brokers, based in London. The immediate results of the merger were that Willis now had an extensive US network of branch offices, and Corroon & Black's international network became stronger and larger, including new offices in Eastern Europe and Russia. Company employees reacted to this major development with mixed feelings. Some thought positively, thinking that the merger would allow C&B to grow and would make the company stronger. Others were concerned about their jobs in the near future. In coming weeks and months, some employees, including senior executives, left the firm. The transition lasted a long time, eventually ending during a bad economic slump that greatly affected Japanese US investments. Nineteen ninety-three was a bad year for new Japanese business production for my unit, and I was not sure how long the downturn would last. Meanwhile, as part of the organization's restructuring of CBI's operations, a major change in management occurred at the home office. A new managing director replaced the international department's president, and he proceeded to make various changes, including shutting down my San Francisco Japanese unit as of June 30, 1994. I thought this office closure was penny wise and pound foolish, and I was not alone in this assessment. I tried to salvage my Japanese unit, but it was to no avail. It was, however, déjà vu for me, as I'd been through a number of such corporate restructurings in the past. But this time, it was different. I happened to be behind the eight ball!

CHAPTER 18
Japanese Consultant

By the time Tania and I returned to San Francisco from our Moscow summer vacation at the end of June 1994, my contract with Willis Corroon International had ended. I turned in my corporate-leased Sable station wagon, replacing it with a new Saturn sedan I had purchased from a dealer near my home. I bid my faithful administrative assistant, Midori Kamesato, sayonara and best wishes, as she would also be seeking new employment. (Fortunately, she shortly found a new position at a Japanese firm on the San Francisco peninsula.) Looking back, the seven and a half years I spent working for Corroon & Black International were some of my happiest and most productive years. This was especially true in respects to the earlier years, when I was busy setting up CBI's Japanese network. I enjoyed working closely with C&B's friendly and energetic Pacific construction division team members, as well as with the brokerage service group staffers from the western states, all of whom were involved with our various Japanese business production campaigns. I had made friends at the various offices, and it was a pleasure to travel with them to the numerous Japanese firms we dealt with. I remember fondly the annual sales visits to Tokyo, when I accompanied the construction division's representatives to Tokyo and other regions. The planning and staging of C&B's first ever construction insurance seminar at the Tokyo American Club was a memorable, as well as a successful, project. My unit and our Tokyo correspondent office played a key role in ensuring the success of that seminar. It gave C&B's construction division high visibility among the Japanese contractors and insurance underwriters. In fact, the Japanese-language booklet that we had prepared, "Construction Insurance/Bonding in the US," was a big hit with Japanese construction companies interested in doing business in the United States.

Earlier in the spring, I had heard of a European-based insurance brokerage firm that was planning to open a new Japanese business division in Los Angeles and San Francisco. It sounded like a good and timely opportunity for me, so I contacted the LA headhunter who was in charge of finding qualified bilingual staff for the new venture. He had already been talking to a number of Japanese and Japanese American insurance agents in Los Angeles, and was pleased to hear from me regarding the San Francisco slot. I forwarded my resumé, plus some additional data, to him, and eventually met with the principals.

As it turned out, the vacancy was an insurance sales position, without the kind of team support that I had had at my previous job. Also, the new business revenue expected annually by this start-up venture was quite significant. As a Japanese resource, I did not own a book of business that I could transfer to my new employer, so any business I acquired would have to be from scratch. It would also require a considerable period of time to produce. I needed to take into consideration as well that I was bound to a two-year non-compete contractual obligation to my former employer. This meant that for two years, I could not solicit any of the business I helped produce for CBI. It wasn't hard for me to contact new Japanese prospects or to deal with the Japanese underwriters who controlled a significant volume of their group-related business. The problem was that my new employer was new to the local American-based Japanese-business environment. Name recognition is very important in the Japanese-related financial services business sector, and a successful track record of dealing with Japanese clients is crucial. Japanese insurance clients do not often change insurance brokers, but when they do, they perform significant due diligence before making their new pick. My new firm would have to make a mark for itself before it could become a recognized broker in the Japanese business community. This was my dilemma when I signed up as a vice president of this new operation. In any event, and in retrospect, it appears the new Japanese business venture was doomed right from the start. Most likely, it was because the company was not in a position to make a long-term investment commitment, as they apparently were interested in quick, profitable returns on investments. Secondly, the timing was not good. Japanese investments, which had been booming in California and elsewhere in the States, had literally dried up. If it was difficult for the major, long-established insurance brokers, with a history of doing business with

Japanese corporations in the United States, to win new business at the time, imagine how more difficult it was for a new organization. In short, my employment with this firm lasted less than a year. Shortly after, the rest of the Japanese business division, plus the remaining non-Japanese business divisions, were sold.

After the above fiasco, I decided to end my corporate insurance business career and become my own boss. I did some due diligence of my own vis-à-vis the possibility of opening my own insurance agency, but decided not to pursue this avenue for a number of reasons. I could have acquired a major or minor stake in an existing agency, but it would have required a significant long-term commitment, which I wasn't prepared to make. Also, quite a number of insurance agents and brokers who were my age and had their own agencies, were actually selling or thinking of selling their businesses. My discussions with them didn't provide me with any optimism. Bottom line, I decided owning and operating an insurance or brokerage business was for the younger generation. In my case, and in view of my international background, I decided that my best option was to become an international business consultant, specializing in Japanese, Russian, and Pacific Rim business. After all, these were the areas that I was most interested in and in which I had considerable experience.

The first thing I did as a new international business consultant was to mail an introductory letter to all of my contacts in the insurance industry, as well as to selected insurance companies that I thought might be interested in my background and experience. While the response from them was not what I had hoped for, I did hear from some of the insurance company executives, including a few with whom I was personally acquainted. That was enough to jump-start my new operation. After that, I was often contacted by insurance-related organizations, for which I would troubleshoot sticky problems that they were experiencing with their associates in Japan. Having worked in Japan for many years and fluent in the language, I was able to solve their problems to their complete satisfaction. My clients often told me that they were under the impression that some things just couldn't be done (or fixed) in Japan. I proved them wrong in every situation. As a consultant, I also undertook various projects assisting clients with their international insurance marketing studies, including one in China. One of the more exotic places I was invited to provide technical know-how assistance to was a short-term insurance agency project in Kazakhstan (an oil-rich former member country of the Soviet Union). Unfortunately, I was not able to accept. I enjoy working with people from all over the world; and from time to time, I have been called to interpret at international business meetings, not only in Japanese, but occasionally in Russian. As a result, I have met a lot of interesting businesspeople, including representatives of non-profit organizations, retired civilian, military, and government officials. I've enjoyed working with all of them. Consulting is a two-way street. While assisting my clients with their projects, I was also learning a lot from them. This, I found very stimulating.

I am often asked by young people about the opportunity of working in Japan. Before I reply, I ask them about their interests, and what they would like to see and accomplish by living and working in Japan. Much depends on whether they plan to work for an American company as an expat employee, or for a Japanese firm as a local hire. I advise my young friends that before going to Japan, they should first complete their college education and gain experience working in the United States in their chosen field. Only after they have a solid educational and work experience behind them, should they apply to an American firm for an expat's position in Japan. (Unless they are lucky to have a corporation hire them straight out of college and train them for an overseas position, a rather unlikely possibility nowadays.) Only when you are well trained, should you travel to Japan. When you eventually return to the States, it will be easier to find a job in your chosen field with the added international experience. On the other hand, if you choose to go to Japan to work for a Japanese company or organization, be very careful. Generally, Japanese companies do not hire gaijins in their regular corporate structure. They usually employ them as special assistants or consultants to assist the Japanese firm in some specific field or department, often as English writers or editors. In most cases, there aren't any career opportunities, and the job often is of limited duration. The monthly salary frequently is not adequate, considering how expensive it is to live in Japan. However, if you are an adventurous sort and are thinking of going to Japan on a working holiday, you can always go there to teach English. The Japanese are eager to learn English from native speakers, and there are hundreds of English language schools in Japan, all keen to hire native English speakers. But be very careful not to end up working for a fly-by-night operator, as there are those kinds of language schools as well. Reputable English schools in Japan that offer decent salaries and limited benefits exist, but you must always consider the high cost of living in Japan. A key factor to take into account would be housing costs. The kind of accommodations you need might be totally out of your price range. In short, do your homework before accepting a job in Japan—or in any other foreign country, for that matter.

The Lavrov family, South Lake Tahoe, February 16, 2010.

CHAPTER 19
Epilogue

When I first left Japan at age sixteen, little did I dream that I would return in a professional capacity, eventually becoming a Japanese business sensei. But fate follows its own course. I also never planned or imagined a career in insurance. It was probably my first five-year expat assignment at J&H Tokyo that spurred my interest in working with the Japanese. When I followed it up with another five and a half years representing Chubb in Japan, I was hooked. From then on, doing business with the Nihonjin (Japanese) became my specialty. It also became my springboard for the rest of my business career. Actually, I was initially introduced to the world of Japanese corporate business in San Francisco. As I outlined in an earlier chapter, even before I left San Francisco on my first international assignment to Tokyo, I was already working with a number of J&H San Francisco representatives on a project to obtain new Japanese accounts in the Bay Area and Northern California. At that time (late 1974 into early 1975), my associates and I would often meet with Japanese businessmen working for major Tokyo-based trading houses. In order to break the ice with these gents, we often would ask them about the three s's. Japanese expats knew the answer and would immediately say, Sydney, Singapore, and San Francisco. Then, we would ask them if they'd been to Sydney or Singapore, and how those places compared with San Francisco. This opening small talk helped establish communication with our Japanese prospects and paved the way for more serious discussion. The three s's referred to the countries that were the most popular Japanese expat posting locations during the 1950s-1970s.

At about the same time, I joined the Japanese Chamber of Commerce in San Francisco; and later, the Japanese Chamber of Commerce of Southern California in Los Angeles. Attending their monthly meetings and events provided me with an excellent opportunity to meet and to get to know locally-based Japanese businessmen. Just as I later found the American Chamber of Commerce in Japan (ACCJ) very helpful when working in Tokyo, the California-based Japanese chambers introduced me to many Japanese movers and shakers and their California-based companies. One of the most useful business activities sponsored by these chambers was the quarterly new members cocktail evening, where we had the opportunity to meet and exchange meishis (business cards) with new and current members. I remember handing out no less than forty of my cards and receiving the same number in return at each of these functions.

In more recent years, and as I continued working with my Japanese clients and prospects, I also started to take an interest in the emerging Russian business environment. In the mid 1990s and later, many Russian trade delegations visited San Francisco. Some of us in the Russian-American community decided it would be a good time to establish a local Russian-American chamber. With support from the venerable Russian Center and some other local Russian-American organizations, a San Francisco-based chamber was incorporated in late 1993, and I was elected as its first president. It was a start-up organization, and we worked hard to attract new corporate and individual members and supporters. We published a quarterly newsletter and arranged numerous functions, including VIP welcome receptions, speaker's forums, and other activities of interest to the members. I was honored to serve as its president for two years (1994–1995). I have remained a member in a number of non-profit organizations to stay active and network with the members. I enjoy meeting some of our local St. Joseph alumni group members, to stay in touch and remember the good old days we spent in Yokohama. Sadly, the school closed in 2000 after one hundred years of service to the foreign community in the Yokohama/Tokyo area, and our alumni list gets shorter as the years roll by. Just a few of my friends and classmates that come to mind who have passed away include Serge Bielous (SJC class of 1933), Victor Minenko (SJC class of 1954), and George Bellikoff (SJC class of 1961).

As with Victor and George, Serge Bielous was a friend of our family. My mother, originally from Ukraine, was acquainted with his mother, who also hailed from the Ukraine. I remember during the early postwar years, when I used to follow my mother everywhere, my mom and I would visit the Bielous family home, which was located in front of the Ferris Girls High School on the Bluff. Mrs. Bielous was such a sweet hostess, and in the summertime, she always treated me to an ice-cold Coke. In the 1980s, when I was working in Tokyo, I visited Yokohama occasionally. Accompanied by Joe Gordo I would meet with Serge and his wife, Irene, at the Yokohama Country and Athletic Club. Sitting in the club's comfortable bar, we would drink draft beer and have lively discussions of international developments, local Yokohama activities, business, and other items of mutual interest. Our friendly get-togethers always ended with a final "ichi for the michi" round, or one for the road.

Victor Minenko, who lived in Tokyo and was the youngest of six Minenko brothers, was a star basketball player at St. Joseph. Following in the footsteps of his older brother, Leo, he migrated to Australia, where he married Liz Moses, a gaijin from St. Maur's in Yokohama. She and Geoffrey, the youngest of her three brothers, returned to Australia at about the same time I was living in Sydney. Victor Minenko and Paul Bellikoff were roommates at one time in Sydney, and my brother, sister, and I would occasionally join them at their cocktail parties on the North Shore. There were always some Sydney-based Japanese businessmen at these parties, and we spoke a lot in Japanese. It was quite amusing to see the Aussie guests watching us in utter amazement as we spoke fluently with the Japanese corporate representatives.

George Bellikoff and his family lived close to our house on the Bluff. They were dear to our family, and we attended the same church. George, who had two older sisters—Raisa and Elizabeth, or Liz—and one older brother—Alex, who still lives in Yokohama with his family—emigrated to Sydney to join his cousin, Paul Bellikoff. As I heard later, he had been living in Sydney for a long time when he was struck and killed by an automobile while waiting for a tow truck to assist him with his own car, which had broken down on the highway. I will always remember George as a quiet, soft-spoken gentleman.

In recent years, I heard that my childhood friend, Konstantin Kashiloff, whose family moved to the Soviet Union in 1958, was living in Bishkek, capital of the newly independent state of Kyrgyzstan. It appears he has been working there as a university English faculty docent, but my attempts to contact him have been unsuccessful so far.

Though no longer altar boys, as we used to be at the Yokohama Orthodox Church, Paul Uhov, George Belonogoff, and I continue to be close to our new church, the Holy Virgin Russian Orthodox Cathedral in San Francisco. Paul, a longtime church council member, is still our senpai (elder), whom we look up to. He has remained single, and after spending his entire career working for the leading Japanese trading powerhouse, Marubeni (San Francisco), is now happily retired. He continues his volunteer work for SCORE (counselors to America's small businesses), as well as being a docent at the Cathedral. George Belonogoff, after graduating from UC Berkeley, joined the giant San Francisco-based Bechtel Corporation, where he worked until he reached retirement. He and his wife, Elizabeth, have three grown girls and two grandsons (currently living in New Jersey).

As for my family, our oldest son Alex, a construction inspector, is married to Denise, a graphic designer and photographer, and they both are local government agency employees. Nick, our younger son, is a water services inspector. He is married to Belgian-born Geri, and they have a seven-year-old daughter, Sophia. She is a second grader and our pride and joy. After attending Marin Catholic High School for three years, Nick went on to graduate from the University of California, Berkeley with a major in economics. He is also a local government employee, and Geri is an elementary schoolteacher and freelance photographer. My brother Victor is retired and lives with his son, Adrian, an aeronautical engineer, in Albany, Oregon. My sister Tonia and her husband, Reverend Deacon Nicholas Lenkoff, a retired California National Guard officer and Vietnam War veteran, reside in Sacramento, California. Until recently, they also lived in Albany, Oregon, but decided to return to California to be closer to their son, Serge, in Sacramento.

As I am writing this memoir, I am fast approaching the seventy year mark. I never imagined I would reach this milestone, although my father lived until he was ninety-eight, and my mother was ninety-two at her passing. I guess our family's strong old-country genes are helping us stay alive and live healthy and productive lives. Tania and I are happily retired, and we continue to live in Marin County, just north of San Francisco. We continue doing

SJC mega reunion. From left to right, George Belonogoff,
Eric Ebbel, Andrea Fernandez-Cross (Saint Maur's) and I.
Standing behind is Julio Rangel, Los Angeles, February 19, 2000.

our fair share of volunteer work at the church, as well as at
other non-profit community organizations. Domestic and
international travel is also on our horizon. In August 2010,
we embarked on a Baltic Sea cruise from Copenhagen. We
sailed to many northern ports, including St. Petersburg,
where we had a marvelous time, visiting majestic palaces
of the Romanovs, historic churches—including the grand
St. Isaacs Cathedral—and many other interesting and
historic landmarks. Unfortunately, the two days we had
there were simply not enough to do justice to the Empress
of the Baltic, as St. Petersburg is nicknamed. During our
stopover in Stockholm, we met with Ingrid Johansson, my

friend from early San Francisco days. I had not seen Ingrid for almost fifty years, but I recognized her right away. Her warm smile and bubbly personality hadn't changed. Although it was raining that day, Ingrid led us on a wonderful tour of Stockholm, which is a beautiful capital city, with its myriad of waterways, historic churches, well-maintained government buildings, beautiful parks, and, of course, charming people.

Looking back, except for the World War II period and the early postwar years in Japan, I've led a good life. Thanks to my early education at St. Joseph and the support I received during my career, I was able to succeed in international business and enjoy a comfortable life, including living overseas for ten and a half years. I am also glad I made the choice to come to America and become an American citizen. I have been a longtime member of the Congress of Russian-Americans, a heritage organization based in San Francisco, and remain a proud Russian-American.

Since my early stateless White Russian days growing up in Yokohama, and later as an American expat working in Tokyo, I have spent half a lifetime interacting with the Japanese. You might say I've gotten to know them well. In fact, I've often been mistaken for Japanese, especially while speaking Japanese on the telephone. Times have changed, yet in one respect, they have remained constant. The perception of the Japanese vis-à-vis the foreigner is the same as it was many years ago. Kipling, the famous British writer of the nineteenth century, was right when he penned, "Oh, East is East, and West is West, and never the twain shall meet ..." Over the years, I have witnessed many gaijins, including Americans young and old, attempt to become Japanese. They study the language and immerse themselves in Japanese customs and traditions, marry Japanese spouses, and some even work in Japanese firms. And yet, after a lifetime of effort, were they really accepted as Japanese by the natives? Have the close-knit Japanese, in general, tried to integrate foreigners into their society? The answer, in my view, is no. While the Japanese are keen to trade and interact with foreigners, they are not prepared to transform their homogeneous society into a multicultural nation, like the United States or Brazil. Once a gaijin, always a gaijin! That's exactly how I experienced living in Japan, as has, no doubt, most every other foreigner who has lived or continues to live in Japan. It's the Japanese way, and you can bet on it! Still, having lived the life of a gaijin, in the words of the famous French chanteuse, Edith Piaf, I can honestly say, "Non, je ne regrette rien." (No, I do not regret anything.)

Practical Dos and Don'ts of Etiquette in Dealing with the Japanese

Dos

- Always be punctual.
- Do your homework.
- Always be patient.
- Always start with small talk.
- Listen.
- Be courteous.
- Be persistent.
- Always write prompt thank-you letters.
- Always use last names.
- Always carry sufficient business cards.
- Always pay the bill.

Don'ts

- Don't be funny.
- Avoid slang.
- Don't promote yourself. Always emphasize your company. Wear your firm's badge.
- Don't appear "out of the blue."
- Don't dress oddly. (The nail that sticks out must be hammered in.)
- Never make unachievable promises.
- Don't do business by phone or pencil only. Make as many personal calls as possible.
- Don't mix-up business titles.
- Don't stare directly into someone's eyes.
- Avoid giving gifts that are not properly wrapped.

Harbin, China

Vladivostok, Russia

Yokohama, Japan Tokyo, Japan

Shanghai, China

Sydney, Australia

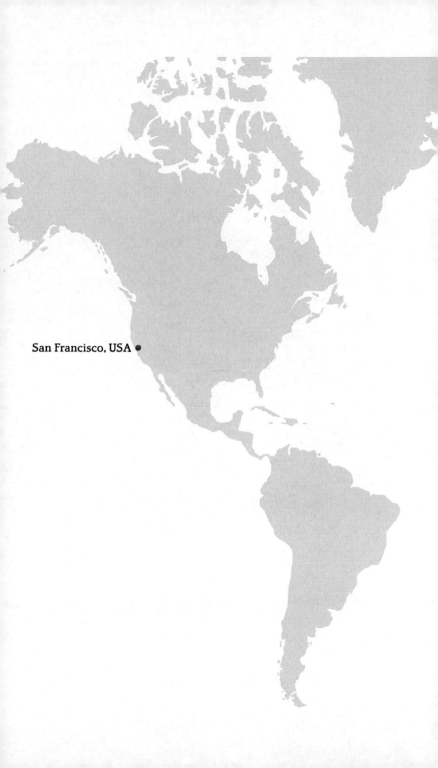
San Francisco, USA

TO MR. LAVROV

FROM J & H JAPAN

J&H Tokyo Sayonara Card.

J&H Tokyo Sayonara Card signatures.

A W A R D

T H E,

Robert F. Corroon

is presented to

George Lavrov, C&B of San Francisco

for dedication and commitment to providing the highest
quality professional service and for outstanding
production excellence in 1989.

Robert F. Corroon
Chairman of the Board
Corroon & Black Corporation

J. Bransford Wallace
Chairman
Brokerage Services Group

CORROON & BLACK

Corroon & Black Achievement Award

RUSSIAN-AMERICAN
Marketplace

blished by the Russian-American Trade and Commerce, Inc.   Jan 1995

New '95 Board Announced - Lavrov Re-elected President
New Chamber Name Adopted
San Francisco

The Russian American Chamber of Commerce in San Francisco, Inc., is pleased to announce that at the Annual General Meeting of the chamber held on January 19, 1995, the following Officers were elected for 1995:

President: George Lavrov
Insurance Broker
1st V. P. : Hans Loken
M.D.
2nd V.P.: Antonina Pushkarow
Consultant
3rd V. P.: Tatiana Roodkowsky
Lawyer
Secretary: Vladimir Belaeff
Consultant
Treasurer: Linda Tern
Office Manager

Also, the chamber has changed it's name to "RUSSIAN AMERICAN TRADE & COMMERCE INC." This change was necessitated to distinguish the organization from the myriad of "Russian-American" chambers of commerce and other trade organizations that have been established recently.

RUSSIAN AMERICAN TRADE & COMMERCE INC. was established in 1993 and it's mission is to (1) represent and assist the Rus-

sian-American business community, (2) promote commerce between the U.S. and Russia, (3) enhance the education and involvement of Russian-Americans in domestic and international business and (4) participate in the development of a free-market economy in Russia.

GOALS AND OBJECTIVES
RATC's Goals and Objectives are

as follows:

• Represent and promote the professional interests of Russian-American entrepreneurs, small businesses, corporations and the Russian-American community in the United States.

• Maintain a close, working relationship with the Russian Consulate General in San Francisco.

continued on page 6

Speaker's Forum
Vladimir S. Kuznetsov
Russian Consul General

Transact your business in Russian and you won't have to fear competition from any trade organizations and ultimately, success will be yours. So declared Russian Consul General in San Francisco, Vladimir S. Kuznetsov, at the Quarterly Speaker's Forum held on December 1st, 1994 at the Russian Center. Speaking candidly and recalling his first meeting with chamber representatives about a year ago, when he suggested the chamber adopt Russian as it's "working language", Mr. Kuznetsov underscored the im-

portance of language in developing new business opportunities. It is now time for the chamber to assess it's priorities, said Mr. Kuznetsov. For example, "What are your goals and what differentiates your chamber from the other organizations promoting business with Russia? What advantages do you offer and what do you expect to achieve? And (in reference to the various "Russian-American" chambers and other groups that have sprung up here in recent years), cooperation and not con-

continued on page 7